An Unlikely Cornish Fisherman

The Early Years

Michael Soady

Table of Contents

Dedication

This is dedicated to my eldest daughter Deborah. Without her persistent requests for me to put "pen to paper", this story would never have been written.

From left to right: Dena, Michelle, Deborah, Yvette, and Lucy

Acknowledgements

I would like to thank the Board of Commissioners of the "East and West Looe, Harbour and Bridge" Charity, for their permission to access the Looe Harbour Archives.

About the Author

Michael Hugh Soady was born at West Looe, Cornwall, on 19 September 1937, the eldest son of a 6th Generation Fisherman Fernley Soady and his wife Edna May (nee) Toms. Michael was educated at Looe School, Liskeard Grammar School and Devonport Engineering College. He was conscripted for National Service, serving as a Non-Commissioned Officer in the Corps of Royal Military Police for two years from February 1960 – January 1962.

Prior to "call up", 1959 – 1960, and after demobilisation 1962 – 1969, he was the sole Electrical/Electronic Draughtsman employed by the Superintendant Armament Supply Officer for the Admiralty at the Royal Naval Armament Depot, Ernesettle, Plymouth. On 2 July 1969, Michael joined the crew of his fathers` fishing boat, "Endeavour" (FY 369), eventually buying the boat from his father in September 1972.

Michael has served two four year terms as a Looe Town Councillor (holding the post of Deputy Mayor 1985/86); in addition to two terms as a Trustee of the local Charity, East Looe Town Trust.

In April 1971, Michael became a member of the ten-man Board of Looe Harbour Commissioners, being elected as Chairman for the first time in November of 1973. During the intervening years from 1971 to 1990 and 1999 to 2019, he was elected to the Commissioners in 13 tri-annual, public elections, serving four years as Vice Chairman and 17 years as Chairman during his time on the Board of Commissioners. He was Chairman in 2019, during his final year as a Commissioner and the oldest serving Chairman of the Board of Looe Harbour Commissioners at age 82. Michael has now retired from Public office.

Introduction

East Looe Sea Front, 1920

I was born prior to the outbreak of WWII in the local Nursing Home (known as Nurse Parker`s), Dorien House, Beech Terrace, West Looe Cornwall, on Sunday 19 September 1937. I was only made aware of the nature of my coming from my mother during a conversation when she was in her late 80`s. She said on that "fateful" Sunday, I had ruined my father`s Sunday lunch! We lived close to East Looe beach in a small two up, two down cottage at Lower Chapel St., East Looe ( commonly called the "back streets") and I suppose the significance of my mother`s remark was that my father, being a fisherman, was hardly ever home to a Sunday lunch! My mother said that when her labour pains started, she had to leave the Sunday lunch unfinished and trek the three-quarters of a mile, mainly uphill, to the

Nursing Home. I was delivered at 4:00 pm. I asked my mother why she chose the name "Hugh" for me, as it was not a family name and unfashionable. This name caused me no end of "ribbing" throughout my young life. My mother replied proudly that she had named me after her first employer, a retired Army Colonel Hugh McKenzie.

My first memories.....The "Black out" and someone shouting, "Put that light out!" ....the unlit `back streets` during wartime....sleeping under the sitting-room table for several weeks....barbed wire at the entrances to Church End and the Seafront.....standing on the seafront with my mother watching the fire glow over the Rame head as Plymouth burned during the blitz, the last raids were in 1944. The search light positioned at the Harbour entrance.......Gun emplacement at the eastern end of the Sea front.....going to day school at Miss Crouch`s house on the Seafront, so my mother could go out to work with my father at sea most of the time. (I was about 3 – 4 years old, and my mother paid Two Shillings a day for me to attend.) ......Bread and butter at My Gran Soady`s (my father`s mother) ....listening to my Gt. Grandfather Thomas Toms relating his outrageous stories about when he was the last coxswain of the rowing and sailing lifeboat " Ryder".......(In later years, I read the Log of the "Ryder" and his stories were all the true facts of the lifeboats rescues.)...Defying my mother by climbing on the static water tank in the Old Market Square.........my mothers` long-handled wooden spoon (I called her `jam spoon`) which she stirred the washing in the "copper" clothes boiler......and also chastised me with it, each time I "misbehaved!"....knocking on the back door of ferryman Sammy Symons to see if he had any marbles which he occasionally found in the river at low tide........... Ronnie Chalk`s `gang`....and him firing an arrow in my left eye during a game of "Cowboys and Indian" in 1942.......many visits to Plymouth eye infirmary (which at that time was an all-day railway excursion)

Samuel Simmonds

.....Not understanding why I was "farmed" out to my Aunt Phoebe for three weeks.... reason..... My brother Alan being born in 1942.........winter time... "Pipe roaring"...stuffing newspaper up drain pipes and setting the paper alight., the up draught causing a very loud roaring, alarming the occupants of neighbouring houses....getting caught and being "clipped" around the ears by Sergeant Bellamy............ In the street we called "Dustbin Alley", tying as many metal dustbin lids together with one another and then tying the last one to the door handle of the last house in the street....then knocking on the door, running away, and waiting at the end of the street for the resounding noise of multiple dustbin lids crashing to the ground when the unsuspecting occupant of the end house open the door. ...climbing the cliff at Plaidy Beach to get at a Kestrels` nest......failed miserably several times!

Dustbin Alley... the adjacent "Backstreet" to where I lived

........my small garden at the top of Bay View Road, my cousins` husband let me have a small area of land to plant vegetables.......my love of gardening......buying a penny fizzy drink at my Aunt Maud's shop at Church

End......collecting discarded lemonade bottles from the beach and returning them to Aunt Maud for a return of two pence each..........getting chastised many times with my mother`s "jam spoon" for playing football on the beach in my "school" shoes.....repeatedly sliding down "Skiddery Rock" and tearing a hole in my trousers......further chastisement with the "Jam spoon"........the ignominy of having to wear the trousers to school the next day with a huge patch on the rear end!.......noticing for years, a small boat lashed to the rafters in the store my father had in the Seafront Albatross building (The Building was once a Pilchard "Palace", where the fish were processed for export).........the boat was my mothers` called the "Hilda"...........spending hours with two old fisherman...a local...Steve Cox ......and a Belgian refugee Fisherman.....Albert Daems....who was crew on my father's fishing boat "Endeavour!"........walking all the way to school at West Looe, home for lunch, back to school in the afternoon and home again after school.......my inherent dislike of school, which lasted all through my youth,.......my burning ambition to be a Fisherman...... going to sea occasionally with my father aboard the "Endeavour".........catching a conger eel in the Looe Angling festival off the Banjo Pier......the conger taking a `liking` to the index finger of my right hand.....the pain as the doctor stitched the end of my finger back together....... the misery of passing the 11+ exam a year early.......daily travel on the steam train to and fro to Liskeard Grammar School ....these are just a few random recollections that have spurred me on to enlarge on these memories and to try and make some sense of them (Before I forget!).

Banjo Pier, October 2014

My story is probably similar to some of my contemporaries, but as I have been the proud owner of 11 boats, I have used the boats as the basis of my stories, and I have tried to fill in the `blanks`.

19 September 1947 - 8 June 1963

Chapter 1: The "Hilda"

Me and the "Hilda" July 1953

The Hilda was a 13ft clinker-built rowing and a sailing boat built of elm planking on oak timbers (ribs), probably built in Looe by Richard (Dick) Pearce. My mother, Edna, was "in service" from 1923, at the age of 14, to retired Army Colonel McKenzie, whose residence was at Shutta Road, East Looe,

My mother, Edna May Soady (and her friend Mable Dingle) rowing the "Hilda" in the summer of 1935

She even gave me my middle name after the Colonels` Christian name, Hugh; she told me that she had bought the boat from the Colonel in October 1933 for the princely sum of £3.00.

(Looe Harbour Commissioner records confirm the date of the purchase)

From as early as I can remember, I always wanted to have a boat and be a fisherman like my father, my grandfathers and my grandfather`s grandfathers. I was born into a family where generations of fisherman were on both my parents` sides, so I guess it was in my blood. With the cessation of hostilities in World War II, the Looe fishing boats were allowed complete freedom to resume unrestricted fishing operations. An admiralty licence was required by fishermen to allow them to fish and only in certain sea areas during wartime. With the war at an end, at a very early age, my father allowed me to go to sea on his 35ft fishing boat, the "Endeavour" (FY369), at every chance I had; albeit, the weather had to be fine. I suffered extreme "mal de mer"; in fact, the affliction haunted me all through my seagoing career. I have various recollections of the change of fishing operations as the seasons changed all those years ago. The excitement of leaving port in the early hours of the spring and summer mornings to go crabbing; the anticipation of waiting for each crab pot to come aboard to see what it had trapped; a lobster, sometimes several hen crabs (which the fishermen called "bun crabs"), sometimes a huge cock crab, spider crabs (The Looe fishermens` name for them was a `skerry`.) the odd conger eel, pouting, cuckoo wrasse or ballan wrasse that had entered the pot to steal the bait; the variation was exciting and endless. The thrill of leaving port early after lunchtime in the winter to drift net fish for pilchards was always there with me. The incredible sight of a shoal of silvery pilchards all meshed by their heads, interspersed with the odd herring and mackerel, as the nets were manhandled inboard. Going to school, to me, was just an imposition and each day to be got through as quickly as possible. My mind made up. I *would* be a fisherman. Each time I mentioned this to my father and offered to be his crew when I was older, his reply would always be the same: ***"Get yer skoolin` ma sonny, then ya can get a proper job."***

I remember September 1947 as being warm and dry, and in fact, records show that as late as the 15th and 16th, temperatures reached near 29C. September went on to be the 20th warmest on records dating back to 1659.

My 10th birthday, Friday the 19 September, was also a warm and sunny day and walking home from school in the late afternoon, my thoughts dwelt on the weekend ahead and what I was going to have for my birthday tea. Would I have a real birthday cake this year as the food was more plentiful, two years after the end of the war? I walked along the quayside and noticed that the Endeavour was missing from her berth; dad was at sea again. Would I have to go to my grandma`s house, who lived across the street, to wait until my mother arrived home from work? There was no surprise to find the front door open when I arrived home. We never locked any doors. In fact, I can`t recall having a key to the front door. Our house was the only house this side of Lower Chapel Street that had front and back doors. It was a nice surprise to find my mother at home, and the front room table was laid for tea. My brother Alan, five years my junior, was there and my fathers` mother, who we called Gran Soady.

She was actually called Mary. Her husband Edwin (Ned), my grandfather, had sadly died in February. I opened a number of birthday cards and the only present I can remember from that day was a brown ten-shilling note given to me by Gran Soady. We sat down to luxurious ham sandwiches followed by my mother`s homemade apple pie and homemade cream. (No fish, thank goodness) Another surprise was an iced birthday cake with ten lit candles, which I can still remember only blowing out 9 with my first puff. (Sugar and sweets were rationed during WWII. It was not until September 1953 that sugar rationing ended)

The "Albatross" building and "Little Beach"

After we had a piece of birthday cake, my mother led us all out to the seafront where my father had a net store in the "Albatross" building, which he leased from East Looe Town Trust. She unlocked the padlock, opened the door and invited us all into the gloomy store. My mother said, "*Here is your birthday present*". In front of my eyes was a boat that seemed to fill the store, painted yellow inside and out with brown gunwales (pronounced gunnels), a red anti-fouled bottom, brown cross stern thwarts and brown bottom boards. A pair of varnished oars, with rowlocks, a varnished boat hook, a rudder and tiller, a `grape` anchor and chain, anchor rope, a foremast on which a white canvas lug sail was hoisted and a brown painted name board in which the name "HILDA" was carved and picked out in yellow paint. This was the same Hilda that my mother had purchased from Colonel McKenzie so long ago. The boat had been strapped upside down to the roof rafters in the store for eight years. I was overwhelmed with joy, excitement; to this day, I have no recollection of any conversation in those moments of utmost ecstasy. I was brought down to earth when my mother told me that I would not be allowed to use the Hilda until the spring of the next year, 1948! Utter ecstasy changed to utter despair, my heart sank. Mother was under strict instructions from my father that I would have to wait until the following spring before Hilda was launched. Later all my pleading and appeals to my father to be allowed to put Hilda in the water, just for this weekend, fell on deaf ears.

I spent most of that weekend in the store, willing the coming winter months to fly by and showing off my boat to my friends or anyone who passed by the store. I remember making plans for the coming year and searching the store, and making a list of things that would come in handy when the Hilda was launched; also, much of the daylight hours in my spare time getting gear ready for fishing from the Hilda. I repaired some of my father's old "Frenchman" crab pots, some cotton Pollack nets, measured lengths of rope for the crab pots, made new dahn buoys while occasionally gazing up at the Hilda; which had the mast taken out and returned to the rafters. I willed the weeks to pass quickly to the next Easter holiday.

In the winter of 1947/48, the weather in December 1947 was mild enough to allow me to work on my gear in the store when I had the time in daylight hours. I seem to recall a tremendous thunderstorm occurring during Christmas afternoon. Except for the natural light coming through the small windows in the store, there was no lighting in the store. I once used a hurricane lamp to light the store, but my father caught me and gave me an `ear wigging` for risking a fire amongst the tinder-dry fishing gear. There was a severe cold spell in the second half of February when it was too cold for me to work in the store. At long last, Easter school half-term arrived. We had arranged the launch date for the Hilda to be on Good Friday as my father would be in from the sea. (He was not happy that I wanted to launch the "Hilda" on a Friday, it was a local superstition that a boat should never be launched on a Friday, I persuaded him by saying it was at Easter and a Religious time, and that outweighed any superstition.) In the preceding weeks, the Hilda was taken down from her rafters "bed" and put outside the store on the top of the lifeboat slipway. She was then partially filled with salt water to tighten up the planking. The Hilda was "clinker" built, where each plank overlaps the one below as distinct from being "carvel" built, where each plank is butted, one to another. The planks in small clinker-built boats are very susceptible to shrinkage when dried out and open up when the boat is kept out of the water for long periods. At first, the water put in the Hilda poured out through the open planks; it took several days, and many buckets of salt water before the planks were tight enough for the Hilda to be safely launched in the river. I spent every spare minute getting all the gear ready for Good Friday.

My recollections of the launch are somewhat hazy. It was about 10 am, and the weather was fine. There was no crowd, no fanfare to watch the Hilda grace the river for the first time in years, just my father, Albert Daems (a Belgian crewman on the Endeavour) and myself. My mother was working. Alan was nowhere to be seen. The three of us dragged the Hilda the short distance down the slipway to the water's edge, I jumped aboard, readied the oars, and my father and Albert slid the Hilda into the river. I still remember the feeling of elation that swept over me as I rowed her on her maiden voyage in my ownership. A short trip out around Riley`s Pier (now commonly known as the "Banjo Pier" because of its shape). I had planned to hoist the sail and see how the Hilda performed in the light breeze; however, she was still leaking, so for safety sake, I decided to curtail the trip and rowed back to the small beach (known locally as "Little Beach".) in the harbour, adjacent to the old lifeboat slipway. Arthur Hosking, the Harbour Master, had given me prior permission to berth my boat on the "little" beach amongst the ferrymen`s rowing boats. I moored the Hilda to a quayside ring and bailed out the water. The Hilda`s maiden voyage complete; not the auspicious occasion that I had dreamed of for all those months, but I still had that feeling of excitement within me. Tomorrow would be another day, the start of another adventure with the Hilda, my very own boat.

I once asked a well-known old fisherman named Alfred John Pengelly (known as AJ) what it was that attracted him to become a fisherman. He paused for a short while, smiled and answered: ***"It`s because of the great uncertainty."***

It was a fact that I came to relate to, time and time again, in years to come.

During the school term following the Easter launch, I became somewhat frustrated because my time was being restricted with the Hilda due to the impending 11plus examination for entry to Liskeard Grammar School. Although I was only ten years old, Mr Burnett, my school form master, recommended that I take the exam a year early, and he offered to give me some private tuition at his home. I was not keen on this at all, and much to my chagrin, my parents agreed, which meant that I would be wasting valuable fishing time at Mr Burnetts` home `swotting` up for an exam that I had little or no interest in taking. This was not part of my well-laid plans for my summer assault on the crabs, lobsters and fish that frequented the waters close to Looe Harbour. At the time, I thought that if I passed, I would have to travel to and fro on the train to Liskeard each school day, which would lessen the time I would have to go fishing in spring and summer. On the day of the exam, I had no motivation or initiative to answer all the questions and taking this exam was just an obstacle in my way to be a Fisherman. So, I have to admit that I did not try to answer all the questions, and I completed my paper ahead of everyone else in the room. Much to my utter surprise and further chagrin, I passed the exam and became the youngest in my class 1A as a student of Liskeard Grammar School in September 1948; the new term was due to start before my eleventh birthday. Another blow to my ambition to emulate my Father.

However, attending Liskeard Grammar School did not damp my enthusiasm to be a Fisherman. In the ensuing years, the Hilda and I became `as one` until she was `pensioned off` in the spring of 1954 when I had the `*Seahorse*` built. Our adventures were varied, and many, sadly most are now lost in the "mists of time". I can only relate to those that remain in my memory after almost 70 years.

Chapter 2: The Summer of 1948

There was a grizzled old fisherman called Steve Cox recognisable from the rear by a shock of white are protruding from underneath his battered peak cap; he must have been 80 years old if he was a day. I always addressed him as Mr Cox. He also had a store in the Albatross building and owned a rowing and sailing boat called the Water Baby, which was painted dark green all over outside and tarred (black) everywhere inboard. During the summer of 1948, I spent more and more time with Steve Cox, learning to splice rope, various knots used for different purposes, net mending, how to make willow `withy` pots and other ideas I could pick from his old brain. One daily event of which I have vivid memories were the races in our boats to see who could sail or row to reach our crab pots first thing in the morning. Thinking back, a ten-year-old vying for supremacy over an 80-year old seems quite bizarre now. Steves` Water Baby was a very heavy clinker-built rowing and a sailing boat that, on close inspection, would not have passed current Health and Safety Regulations. Incidentally, no one at that time wore lifejackets or carried any sort of life preserver in these small inshore boats. Also, most of the fishermen I knew in my youth could not swim. As an inshore crabber, the Water Baby (and others) often came in contact with rocks as they hauled their pots, and she had numerous patches of lead, nailed over brown paper and tar, where she had been on the rocks. It was not uncommon to see his boat upturned on the lifeboat slipway, where Steve could be seen using copper nails to add another tarred lead patch to his boats` already scarred planking.

If there was no wind and we had to row out to our pots, I could hold my own most days in our rowing races. Some days I was first and vice versa. However, I was no match for Steve when there was a breeze of wind; the stronger the breeze, the worse I fared. I could not keep up with that old man in the sailing stakes, although his boat was far heavier than the Hilda. I was so fed up one morning after I was completely out sailed by the old man, added to which I had failed to catch one lobster in any of my 24 pots. I had 24 pots consisting of 4 strings of 6 pots in a string. I could only carry six pots at a time. I shot (placed) the pots in various places, mainly over a rocky sea bed, each pot being spaced 10 fathoms from the next. At each end of the string was a dhan line attached to a dhan buoy on the surface, which enabled me to find where the strings were situated. Steve must have noticed my demeanour, and as we discussed the days catch, I said that I was fed up trying to sail the Hilda in a stiff breeze and losing the race to him time and again. Instead of laughing at me, I remember being amazed when he told me to go to his store and get a 56lb weight. (A half hundred weight). I fetched the weight then he said to get the Hilda alongside. Both of us got aboard, and I rowed outside the harbour. Once at sea, I hoisted and set the sail as he instructed me, all the while he kept explaining how to position the boat in such a way as to make the best use of the wind. He explained that as our boat did not have a drop keel, like real sailing yachts, we could counter that deficiency to a degree by shifting our weight and any other weight to assist the boat's position relative to wind direction. We spent some time sailing up and down, moving our position in the boat, and occasionally I shifted the 56lb weight to where Steve directed. What a difference, the Hilda sailed like a little gem close-hauled to the wind, and Steve also taught me how to set the sail correctly to run before the wind; gone was the side slip when tacking. Lesson over, I moored up the Hilda, thanked Steve profusely for the sailing lesson and went home a lot happier than I was earlier. In the following days and weeks, I can`t say that I beat Steve any more than I had in our previous sailing races prior to my lesson; but I was more confident in my sailing ability and quite often gave Steve close races. I will always hold that knowledgeable old man in high esteem for his tuition and for imparting knowledge to me that I would never get from my future grammar school or my engineering college education.

As the days grew longer in 1948, I would spend some evenings anchoring off the Limmicks rocks to the east side of the Looe harbour, fishing for Pollack and red bream.

Actually, it took me a while and several abortive evenings before I found the right bait, especially for the bream. I was chatting to Steve Cox one evening when I was mooring up the Hilda after another fruitless encounter with the red bream. He asked me what I was using for bait. I told him I had tried pilchard strips, mackerel strips, squid, lug worms (which seemed the best), rag worms and bacon strips. I remember him laughing and saying that I was using the wrong bait, which from my perspective, was pretty obvious. He said that I should get shrimps from the rock pools and use the live shrimps (and prawns) as bait for the red bream. It was the summer holiday, so armed with a bucket and shrimp net. I spent most of a morning scouring the rock pools for shrimps and prawns. The venture was successful. That evening, with the bucket containing a mixture of live shrimps and prawns, the Hilda and I sallied forth to the Limmicks and anchored up. I baited up two hooks with live prawns on a lightly weighted line and let the line run out freely. Normally the weight would touch the bottom, at which time one would reel in slowly, hoping for a bite. This time the line stopped a long way short of the sea bed. It was a bite. I reeled in slowly, fearful of losing what had taken the bait so quickly. Two red bream safely landed, and that was the start of a memorable evening. I used all the live bait, and this time I returned to harbour with a huge grin on my face. I think my catch was 51 red bream. I was in trouble with my mother when I arrived home late. I will always remember her words, *"Where have you been? You have missed supper. Take those boots off. Don`t you know what time it is and you stink of fish..... Go and get yourself washed."* No physical attack with her wooden spoon, just a mild verbal admonishment this time!

The icing on the cake came the next day when I sold the fish to Gilbert Hocking, a local fish buyer. He gave me the princely sum of £1.00. I would never be poor no more. I became quite adept at catching bream, and although I tried to keep what bait I used a secret, eventually, the fact that I was using live bait leaked out to my friends who also had small boats. My supremacy over my friends at bream catching was over. My close friends with their boats were Malcolm Solt (Rosemary), Edward Toms (Pixie), Fernley McVeigh (the boat`s name escapes me), Wren Toms (Francy). Often we all anchored up in close proximity. Competition between us was always fierce in the "angling stakes".

Summer of 1948 was coming to a close, august was almost out, just a few more days, and it would be time to lay up the Hilda in the store for the winter. School beckoned again. One catch still has a special place in my memory, and in my long fishing career, I never saw it repeated again. I had my 24 crab pots in an area close to the east side of Looe Island, a ridge of rocks known as the Rannies, for a few days and the catch of crabs and lobsters were dwindling, day by day. This was a normal phenomenon. I soon learned the first rule of potting, which was that resident shellfish in any given area would be depleted by a sustained fishing effort for any period of time. I decided to move all four strings of pots closer to the harbour in preparedness for taking them in at the end of the season. I made four trips to and from the island, ferrying one string of 6 pots at a time and "shot" each string, after re baiting, closer to the harbour on the Limmicks. The following morning dawned, and much to my horror, the wind was strong southwest, and there was too much sea for me to risk the Hilda in the shallow water over the Limmicks. From the seafront, I could see my dhan buoys in the boiling sea. My fear was that the pots would be damaged or, worse still, smashed up.

The bad weather continued for three days until finally, on Sunday, the weather relented, and it was fine enough for me to get to my pots. I remember it was a Sunday because my mother told me not to forget there was a service at the Methodist Chapel at 11 am, and I was not to be late. There was still a swell when I reached the Limmicks, although the wind had dropped away completely. I decided that now was the time to haul the pots and take them ashore. The crabbing season, for me, was over. This seemed the sensible thing to do as the weather had become unsettled. I remember the relief I felt at finding the first six pots I hauled were all intact and produced four lobsters; I landed the pots on the lifeboat slipway and rowed out for the next string. I repeated the round trip three more times until all 24 pots. Many had sustained damage, dhans and dhan lines were safely stowed on the slipway. I moored up the Hilda in her beach berth and sat in the stern surveying the boxes which held the days` catch in amazement. As I have said previously, my recall after almost 70 years is sometimes open to doubt, but not on this occasion. I had caught 24 lobsters from 24 pots, even though some pots were damaged and empty, which had not been hauled for four days. The number of crabs caught, I cannot remember, no significant number. However, this was a remarkable catch, the most lobsters I had caught in any one day. When I was hauling the pots, I could not believe my eyes. There were four in one pot. I have only seen that twice since that day. Not only that, there were two pots with three lobsters in and several with two in.

In all my excitement, I had completely forgotten Chapel. Later, I suffered the obligatory physical chastisement from my mother by way of her `wooden jam spoon`. On the other hand, my father congratulated me on a fantastic catch of lobsters. A big man of few words, praise from dad was praise indeed. He remarked, *"I hope you didn't tell `anybody!"* It was a fact of life; lobster fishermen never divulged their catch. What to answer when anyone asked if I had caught

any lobsters. As instructed by Steve Cox, I would reply...
"Yes, one with one claw!"

I had covered the Sunday catch with wet hessian sacks in the store, and on Monday morning, I took it on a wheelbarrow to Gilbert Hocking. I cannot recall how much I was paid for the catch. At that particular time, the money was only secondary to the fact that I had caught 24 lobsters in 24 pots. A record I would not best for the rest of my fishing career.

Chapter 3: A Close Run Thing

The 1948 season over, I got a few friends to help me haul Hilda to the top of the slipway adjacent to the store and stowed everything away until next season. I gave Hilda a good scrub, inside and out, and my father and Albert lashed her upside down in her winter berth, high in the rafters. I now had to get ready for the ordeal of travelling to Liskeard by train to start my education at the Grammar school in preparation for the time when I went to get that ***"proper job"*** to which my father always referred.

Fernley Soady (my father)

I should explain to anyone who is reading this that my father Fernley was 6ft 3ins tall and weighed in at 18 stones. One would think a man not to be messed with. He was simply the opposite, an extremely intelligent man of few words; he was the proverbial `gentle giant`. He was completely different to my mother, Edna May, who barely rose to a fiery 5ft in height. I learnt painfully growing up that `armed` with her `jam spoon`, she was certainly not a lady one would wish to cross or to `mess` with.

I still had this inherent dislike of going to Grammar School; to me, it was no more than a chore, and except for the sport, it was a complete waste of my time, and I spent the winter months waiting for spring to arrive so that I could start preparing the Hilda for another assault on the fish living in proximity to Looe harbour. From Easter time onward, I spent most of my spare time getting the Hilda ready for sea. At least my mother was satisfied with my first year at the grammar school as I had finished fourth overall in class from the end of term examination. This was quite surprising to me, really, because I had done the bare minimum of homework and the majority of that on the train to and from school. Summer arrived at last! I spent most of the six weeks holiday having so much fun, sailing and fishing aboard the Hilda; then, much to my dismay, it seemed that no sooner had it started, the holiday was over.

The summer of 1949 had come and gone, September had arrived, and it was back to school for the Autumn Term to start my 2nd year as a pupil of Liskeard Grammar School. I was the youngest in my class, Form 2A. As it turned out, weather-wise, it had been a very fine summer and notably one of the top 7 warmest years of the 20th Century. The "Hilda" was now safely put away again for the winter in my father`s store in the Albatross Building at East Looe seafront, which also accommodated a further six fisherman`s stores.

However, I had come up with a great Idea but, my father`s saying. *"It was a good idea that should remain an idea!"* was incessantly ringing in my ears.

Throughout the summer, I had noticed large shoals of grey mullet and bass travelling up the river on the flood tides and congregating in the West River close to the Cornish Canners Pilchard Canning Factory, which was situated at Polean, West Looe. I had an idea, or at least the embryo of an idea, which was slowly emerging into a "*cunning plan*".

There were reports of anglers catching Bass and Grey Mullet whilst fishing off the river bank where the employees of the Canning Factory dumped all the Heads, Guts and Tails of the Pilchards after the fish was processed. The more I thought about all these fish ready and waiting to be caught, the more I concluded that a 4-inch mesh net stretched across the river at the right state of the tide could reap a substantial "silvery" financial reward. However, there was a snag!

“Shooting” nets in the Looe River was banned by the Looe Harbour Commissioners [unless permission was granted], and furthermore, a licence was required to catch Sea Trout and Salmon, which frequented the upper reaches of the East and West Rivers.

During the Liskeard Grammar School October half-term, I spent time at the Polean Canning Factory, West Looe, on different days and was amazed at the size of the shoal of mixed Grey Mullet and Bass which were feeding on the discarded pilchard offal dumped from the Cannery. It also became obvious that the feeding period by the fish seemed to cease at a certain state of the ebb tide when the shoal returned to the sea.

I started to put “flesh” on the skeleton of the idea by sharing the plan with my long-time friend Malcolm Solt. Malcolm was a year younger than me, attended Looe School and also had a 12-foot wooden clinker-built punt called “Rosemary”, in which, like I, he went fishing regularly during the summer holiday. I realised that to put the plan into action. We needed a boat and an adequate net. I had a suitable net in the store, but the “Hilda” was strapped up to the rafters in the Albatross store. Hence, I shared my plan with Malcolm because the “Rosemary” was not put in a store; she was hauled up to the top of the old lifeboat slipway next to the Albatross Building, close to our store, and turned up-side-down for the winter!

We had the boat and the net! Now to decide when to implement the plan!

With the warm summer weather past, the nights were drawing in and were getting colder, so I knew if we were going to put the plan into operation, it had to be soon. I checked the tide times over the following days and weeks. An ideal situation; a 6 pm High Water occurred on Saturday, 5 November 1949. Nothing could have worked out better. The original "idea" was materialising; high tide occurring on Guy Fawkes night when everyone would be gathered around their bonfires, eating roast chestnuts, baking potatoes and lighting their fireworks. I could visualise the whole town occupied in their celebrations, whilst Malcolm and I would be up the West River "loading off" the "Rosemary" with bass and grey mullet!

I had purchased a box of mixed fireworks and gave my parents the impression I would be lighting them with my friends around the Bonfire, which was being built on East Looe beach. My mother worked some Saturday evenings at Margaret Dan`s Cafe in Higher Market Street, and my father spent those Saturday evenings [if he was in from sea] playing snooker at the Sailing Club in Buller Street. I realised that if either of them "got wind" of what I had planned, my father being one of the ten Looe Harbour Commissioners, our fishing expedition up the West River would be scuppered.

Malcolm and I made arrangements for our plan. We took his pair of oars and rowlocks for the "Rosemary" and deposited them in our Albatross store along with our wellington boots and two oilskin aprons. We overhauled a sixty fathom Pollack net and mended up any holes that remained from its last haul. These Egyptian cotton nets were vulnerable to rotting if, after use, they were not dried properly when stored until the next season. [*Unlike the nylon and synthetic nets that are in use today*.] I had calculated that the sixty-fathom net would be long enough to reach from shore to shore across the river adjacent to the Canning Factory and deep enough to stop the fish from diving under it. After overhauling the net, we "flaked" it down in a wooden box for ease of carrying aboard the "Rosemary". Finally, we prepared two half hundred weights as end anchors for the net, and two five fathom sisal anchor lines.

We also prepared two hurricane lamps until it dawned on me that on 5 November, there was going to be a full moon; the last piece of the puzzle had fallen into place. We hoped for a clear sky, so we would not have to use the lamps which might highlight our scheme to anyone on shore

Malcolm and I were both pumped up with excitement and anticipation. The few days leading up to 5 November seemed to be endless until finally, Guy Fawkes Day dawned and as luck would have it, the weather was dry and very cold. Everything seemed to be just right for us, even down to a clear blue sky. Malcolm and I spent the morning checking the net and the other equipment. We also wrapped pieces of cloth around the middle of each oar so that no sound would be heard when the oars were in the rowlocks. When no one was around, we turned the "Rosemary" upright and slid her further down the Albatross slipway so she would be close to the waters` edge in the evening. We arranged to meet by the store at 5 pm.

My mother made "tea" for my father, Alan (my younger brother) and me before she went to work at 4 pm. She left after warning me to be careful when lighting my fireworks and not to get too close to the bonfire! With "tea" over, I said, *"I`m off now, see you later!"* A grunt emanated in reply from behind the "Daily Express" newspaper in which my father had his head buried.

I remember feeling exuberant; the time had come to put my "idea" into operation. Malcolm and I arrived at the seafront store at the same time, changed from our shoes into our wellington boots, put the net [in its box], weights and anchor lines, oars and rowlocks aboard the "Rosemary" as well as our oilskin aprons and slid her the few feet to the waters` edge. With no bottom boards, side seats or backboard, the "Rosemary" was light and easy for us young boys to manhandle. Although the star-filled sky was clear and bright with moonlight, we decided to take the hurricane lamps just in case we needed extra light! We left our fireworks in the store, deciding that we would "let them off" when we had finished fishing and had landed our catch! Thinking back to that time, we were certainly not lacking in optimism.

With all the gear stowed aboard the "Rosemary", we launched her off and, taking one oar each, Malcolm and I rowed silently away up the river on the last of the flood tide, the cloth "*wraparounds*" muffled the sound of the oars. Our trip up river was uneventful; we could see a few bonfires alight on the hillsides, and fireworks were "going off" all over town. No one seemed to notice or pay any attention to a small grey punt silently slipping under the bridge and heading up the west river.

When we arrived opposite the Canning Factory, we lay quietly in the calm water and were excited to see the surface of the water rippling with the sign of fish feeding. We continued to lie quietly without speaking until I was sure that it was the top of the tide and the flood tide had finished. Now was the time to get the net in the water before the ebb tide started to make away. I decided that the best way to "shoot" the net was from the Trenant Woods side of the river towards the Canning Factory on the west bank, so we rowed across to the Trenant bank, put on our aprons and prepared the net box in the correct position for "shooting" the net. As we were "shooting" on the top of the tide, I decided not to anchor the net this end as I considered the net would be easier to haul, drifting down with the tide when the ebb started to make away. The evening was very cold with a clear starry sky and good visibility so that we had no need to light the hurricane lamps.

Instead of rowing the boat while we "shot" the net, I stood in the stern and "skulled" the boat slowly ahead using one oar resting on the rowlock in her transom while Malcolm "shot" the net over the starboard side. *[Sculling with one oar over the stern was a way most people used to propel small punts in the Looe River 65 years ago*] This way, I could see where we were going, keeping the "Rosemary" on straight course across the river and I had a point to aim at as someone had lit a bonfire in the garden of one of the Woodlands View Council houses on the opposite bank beyond the Canning Factory.

Everything had gone according to plan; most of the net was in the water, and we were close to the Canning Factory shore when disaster struck!

Whilst Malcolm continued to "shoot" the net. It became snagged, probably on a nail head protruding from the gunwale. Malcolm immediately reacted and lurched across to clear the net; he completely lost his balance and toppled over the side into the river. Instinctively I tried to grab him, but the *`Rosemary`* capsized, and I followed him into the icy water. I can still recall the shock of the cold water as I went under with the boat on top of me. I managed to get to the surface from underneath the boat and was then aware that I had the net tangled around both my legs. It was a peculiar sensation; I had swallowed a great deal of water. All I could think of was that the water was not at all salty! I could hear Malcolm spluttering and splashing around close to me. He was also tangled in the net. The net was slowly dragging both of us under again with the weight of the boat that had started to drift slowly downstream on the first of the ebb tide. I managed to kick my sea boots off, but neither I nor Malcolm could free us from the net, and although I was a good swimmer, I could feel the strength slowly draining from me. I lost sight of Malcolm, and I failed to grab one of the oars as it floated by me. Thinking back, neither of us spoke or even shouted for help. We were both frightened

It was as if I was in a dream; I was going under when a mighty force dragged me backwards until finally, I felt solid ground under me. I was dumped absolutely exhausted, still with part of the net around my leg, onto the river bank. I could hear Malcolm coughing and groaning near me, and I recall retching and trying to get my breath!! A dog was sniffing around me, and I had this recollection of a huge man cutting off the net from around my leg, then asking if I could stand. Shakily I tried to stand, but my legs felt like jelly and gave out under me. The "Giant" kept me upright with one hand under my arm until I regained my equilibrium, and I managed to stand, albeit very shakily, on my own two feet. The "Giant" then lifted Malcolm to stand upright, who seemed worse off than me. Each time he tried to stand, unaided, he collapsed to the ground.

It seemed like a dream. The "Giant" seemed to be saying something like........ *"Come on, let's get you home and dried out*!" He tossed Malcolm over his shoulder and helping me with his other hand. I staggered what seemed an interminable distance to the "Giants" lair! I was so tired. My feet hurt, then I remembered that I had kicked off my boots. The "Giants" lair turned out to be a council house at Woodlands View Estate, and the "Giant" revealed himself to be Jack Moore, a local "fish jowter", later to be a fisherman. It was just pure luck for Malcolm and me that Jack Moore was taking his dog for its evening walk along the river bank by the canning factory. He had stood silently watching us "shoot" the net and had witnessed the catastrophic events as they unfolded.

The house was warm and welcoming; a lady, who we learned later to be Mrs Moore, helped us out of our wet clothes, then wrapped each of us in large towels and sat us in front of a log fire in their sitting room. I remember feeling very shocked and still shivering while attempting to sip a mug of hot, sweet tea, which Mrs Moore had given us. Mrs Moore put more logs on the fire, spread our clothes over a "*wooden horse*", and placed them to dry in front of the fire.

My feet still hurt, and it was then I realised that I had kicked off my boots. My thoughts drifted fearfully. How was I going to explain the loss of my boots to my mother? After warming in front of the fire and downing, the hot tea Malcolm said that he felt a bit better, although he still looked very pale and "*wished*" to me.

When we were warmed, dressed in our dry clothes, and I had stopped shivering, I remember noticing the clock on the mantelpiece chimed on the half-hour and the hour. It was 9 pm. Mrs Moore said that we should run along home now that we were dried off, and she gave me a pair of old slippers to wear. Funny thing, Malcolm kept his boots on when we were in the water; Mrs Moore had almost dried them out with newspaper! We thanked Mrs Moore profusely for all she had done for us and took our leave.

Jack Moore and his van

Jack Moore owned an old red van and was kind enough to drive Malcolm and me to our homes in East Looe. Malcolm lived with his parents and younger sister in a flat at Fore Street over Lloyds Bank, whereas I lived two doors in from St Mary`s Church in Lower Chapel Street, near the Seafront. As he got out of the van by Lloyds Bank, Malcolm agreed we meet at the Albatross store in the morning. There was just a little matter of retrieving the "Rosemary", wherever she was and my net! Jack Moore dropped me off at the seafront, and I retrieved my shoes from the Albatross store. I remember entering our home with trepidation, but my mother just asked me what I wanted for my supper!! One cannot imagine the feeling of relief that ran through me; neither of my parents seemed interested or asked me what I had been doing. My young brother was already in bed, so I declined supper, muttered that I wasn`t hungry and bolted upstairs to the sanctuary of my bed.

Malcolm and I met on Sunday morning at the Albatross store. He had serious grief from his mother because he was late home, but a miracle of miracles; it appeared that neither of our parents had an inkling of our failed fishing expedition the prior evening! The inevitable was yet to happen! The priority was to locate the "Rosemary" and get her back in her berth at the top of the lifeboat slipway before Harold Solt [Malcolm`s father] found she was missing. We searched the harbour from the old lifeboat slipway all the way up to the

Canning Factory, the scene of our failed operation, with no sign of my net or the "Rosemary". Both of us had to return home for Sunday lunch and go to the Methodist Chapel [now a book shop] in East Looe at 2 pm for Sunday school. I remember that when we came out of Sunday school, we were both at our wit's end as to where to find the "Rosemary". We concluded that after we had fallen in the river, the boat had floated out to sea last night on the ebb tide.

Harold Solt

Malcolm had the unenviable task of going home to tell his father of our "bonfire night" escapade and the loss of the "Rosemary". Where I was concerned, I had only lost a net, two hurricane lamps, a couple of half hundredweights, my oilskin apron and worst of all, my wellington boots. However, I was terribly worried about the fallout from the loss of Malcolm`s boat once my parents found out what we had been up to the previous evening.

[*We never found my net; I can only conclude that someone found the net and kept it for themselves; or, maybe Jack Moore had removed the evidence before the Harbour Commissioners had knowledge of our failed fishing trip? Although I put the question to him many times in later life, he would smile but never own up to removing the net from the river.]*

We did not have to wait long before "things" came to a head. Apparently, the "Rosemary" was found washed up on East Looe beach by a lady walking her dog. I will never know to this day how we missed finding the "Rosemary". The lady had reported the find to Arthur Hosking, the Harbour Master; who had contacted Harold Solt and the "*cat was out of the bag.*" Later, Malcolm told me that he was severely punished for taking the boat with a serious loss of pocket money and was "*kept in*" for a week. [*The modern idiom for "kept in" is "grounded"]*. It was my opinion that Malcolm had "*got off*" very lightly!

Arthur Hosking, Looe Harbour Master 1935 - 1957

Malcolm Solt

When I knew that the "Rosemary" had been found intact, I breathed a sigh of relief, although I felt really guilty about the loss as it was my idea to use her. Sunday evening, Harold Solt came to our house and "*outed*" my involvement with the loss of the "Rosemary" to my parents. Very little was said to me until Mr Solt departed, then the wrath of hell descended on me in the form of my mother and her wooden "jam spoon". I did notice, at that time, that my father said very little other than something like: *"You shouldn't have taken her. It wasn't your boat!"* My mother was incandescent with rage and would not be placated, especially over the loss of my wellington boots; the purchase of my new pair of football boots for Christmas was cancelled, and there was a ban on me going to the youth club; a ban on Saturday morning Cinema which was held in the Guildhall [Where the indoor market is now] and I was "kept in" for a month. I was devastated, especially at not having a new pair of football boots. It took the passage of many months and me "grovelling" before peace and calm settled over the "Soady" household.

Endeavour FY 369

Later, both Malcolm and I went to Woodlands View to thank Jack Moore for surely saving both our lives and Mrs Moore for being so caring in the aftermath of the accident. Ironically, almost 20 years later, Jack Moore "shipped up" on my father`s pilchard drifter "Endeavour FY369", of which I was already one of the crew. Jack never tired of reminding me of my aborted bonfire night escapade.

Malcolm and I spent much of our youth together "*messing around*" in our boats; in later years, we rarely spoke of our failed escapade. Malcolm, sadly, is no longer with us. But, during my own rare quiet moments, my thoughts drift back to that fateful Guy Fawkes evening. I am certain that if it was not for the quick thinking of Jack Moore, I would not have my family of 5 great daughters, and both Malcolm and I would have, almost certainly, drowned.

From what started that Guy Fawkes Night, as an explosive idea, ended like a damp squib.

Chapter 4: A Ferryman`s Licence

Each spring, from 1948 to the end of summer 1953, I painted up and refitted the Hilda. I had six summers of real enjoyment with the `old girl`. Each year I shot a few strings of pots, shot nets for Pollack and mackerel, 12" mesh nets for rays and crayfish, long lining, and nighttime angling for conger eels. The choice was endless. The excitement was always there and ***"the great uncertainty***". The financial rewards varied, but I remember I often managed to supplement my `money box`. I entered the under 18 single sculls in Looe regatta each summer but always came second to Wren Toms. One year, Steve Cox told me to lighten up Hilda by removing all seats, bottom boards etc. and black lead the bottom of the boat. Black lead was the stuff that was used to clean the fire grates and stoves. I did all this, and although I gave Wren a good race, I still came second.

For four years, I had rubbed shoulders with the old ferryman who moored their boats at `little beach`. The ferrymen were retired fisherman who now plied their trade carrying passengers to and fro from east to west Looe or vice versa. At that time, much to the consternation of the local populace, the fee to cross the ferry had been raised by 100%, from 1d to 2d. The ferrymen each held a Waterman`s licence issued by the Looe Urban District Council (LUDC), the licensing authority at that time, and they had to pass a competence examination in front of the Harbour Master. I had asked Arthur Hosking, the Harbour Master if I could take the examination for a ferryman`s licence, but he said the minimum age that a person could hold that licence was 14. I reached the eligible age to take the examination on 19 September 1951, so I applied to the Looe Urban District Council, and they accepted my application. I think I jumped the queue at that time. My father was a Looe Harbour Commissioner. I took the test in front of the Harbour Master in early October, which I passed and was issued with my Watermans` license. I think the fee was half a crown (2/6).

I did not want to cause any animosity or take away income from the ferrymen, but I had noticed a small window of opportunity for me to utilise my licence. Looe has a tidal Harbour. The tide ebbs and flows every 6 hours. On the low water of the spring tides, no ferrymen operated the lower ferry from Dungate steps, east Looe to Pennyland slipway, west Looe because their ferry boats were too deep draft. Pennyland was named thus because crossing the river originally at that point cost the passengers 1d. The Hilda was very shallow draft and could float “on wet grass”! I found that I could cross on the lower ferry at the lowest of the spring tides, so I worked the lower ferry whenever possible. I was licensed to carry five passengers, and the best part of operating at the lower ferry was that the water being shallow, I didn`t have to row across. I could walk with my thigh boots on beside the Hilda and just guide her back and forth. I only charged 1d, but I still found it worthwhile financially, and at that time, local people and visitors alike seem to appreciate my innovation, saving them the long walk around the bridge from east to west Looe and vice versa.

I believe I was the youngest person at that time to hold a ferryman`s licence. As a Harbour Commissioner, I had checked past records, and I found no evidence to suggest that I was not the youngest person ever to have held a LUDC waterman`s license. I believe I still hold that distinction.

Chapter 5: Trawling with the Hilda

During the last week in July, all through August 1952, 5 weeks, I was hired as an attendant on the Looe Harbour Commissioners Buller Quay car park, weekdays from 8 am to 5 pm. There was genuine a part-time vacancy, but once again, I was never sure; was I chosen from other candidates because my father was a Looe Harbour Commissioner? I managed to fit my fishing operations around these hours.

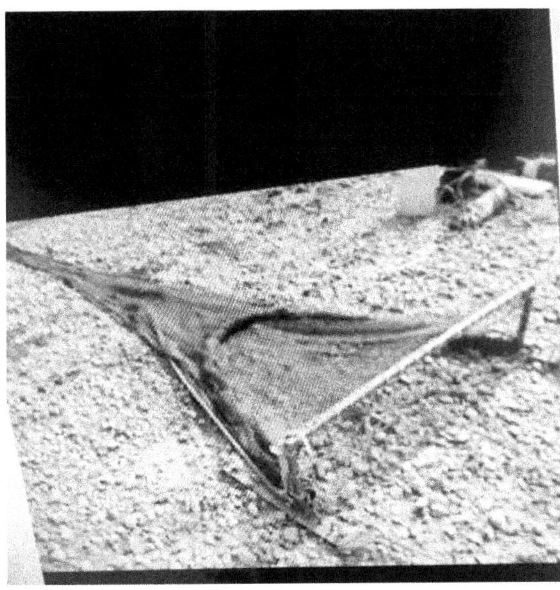

Beam trawl similar to the one I used on the "Hilda" to catch prawns.

I believe that it was August of 1952 when a proliferation of seaweed fouled Looe harbour and the sandy seabed to seaward of the harbour. I had an *idea (all my life, I have never been devoid of ideas!)*. When searching for prawns in the rock pools, one found most prawns hiding under seaweed. I thought that if I could get a small mesh beam trawl, I could tow it behind Hilda to catch any prawns that may be lurking in the seaweed offshore. A beam trawl is a net that is dragged along the seabed. The beam can be made any length, which sits on a triangular steel `shoe` at either end of the beam to keep it above the seabed. In my case, I had an engineer, Jack Stanton, fabricate a 6ft beam from conduit pipe welded on 9 inch shoes. The beam would be 9 inches above the seabed. I needed the net to attach to the beam. I spoke to Albert Daems, who made me a small mesh net out of an old sprat trawl belonging to my father. The net was shaped like a wind sock with the widest end attached to the beam. The narrow end, called the `cod end`, is open and tied up and the knot can be `slipped` to empty the trawl of any fish caught in it. Steve Cox told me that the best time to trawl for the prawns was early evening or in the dark. I had a hurricane lamp which I lashed high up the foremast. In the darkness, the lamp gave out just enough light for me to see what I was doing. Late one evening, I rowed out into the bay and shot the trawl, paying out the 20 fathoms of towing warp which I belayed though the ringbolt fixed to the inside of the transom. On my own, I found this to be a difficult operation as there was no wind to propel Hilda, so there was nothing for it but for me to row as hard as I could to move the trawl along the sea bed. This was not what I had envisaged, having to row. I remember I soon tired, and eventually, the boat came to a halt. I shipped the oars and struggled to haul the trawl from the seabed. The trawl was full of sand and seaweed. Thinking back, I`m amazed at my age what physical strength I had to haul it inboard. I slipped the `cod end` knot the contents flopped out onto the bottom boards. The pile of sand and seaweed became a wriggling and jumping mass. There were prawns in abundance. As the light from the lamp was poor, I decided to return to harbour, and I hitched up beneath a quayside light to clear up the catch. I remember the catch consisted of a full bucket of huge prawns, I think there was also two small plaice, and when I arrived home with the fish and prawns, my mother was so pleased with me (for *a change*). The prawns were a rarity for us. If I recall correctly, we had prawn salad for lunch the next day. Somewhat of a treat, as my father detested salad and tomatoes, luckily for us, he was at sea! I had two more attempts at prawn trawling that week, and I caught a decent amount of prawns, but it was disappointing that nobody wanted to buy them. Although I was quite fit and strong for my age, towing the net by rowing when there was insufficient wind to sail and then having to manhandle the seaweed when the trawl got sanded was just too strenuous for me.

I was chatting to one of my cousins, Shirley Pengelly (sadly deceased), two years my elder, whose father owned the fishing boat `Renee` and related my trawling experiences. She was interested, and as she was a strong oarswoman, she offered to come out with me and help me tow the trawl. We arranged to go one evening before the new school term started, and the Hilda was put away for the winter, but the weather was inclement for several days. So, I came up with another great idea! Shirley agreed to come with me. It was early September, so the idea was to tow the trawl up the west river on the first of a flood tide, and the idea had to be implemented soon before we went back to school and the Hilda went back in the store. There was a complete ban on using nets in Looe Harbour unless one had the Harbour Master`s permission. I reasoned, wrongly as it subsequently turned out, that as my father was a Harbour Commissioner and I had worked for the Commissioners recently on their car park, it would be alright for me to trawl up the river.

I had checked that the west river bed was clear of obstacles from where the west river met the east river at Trenant Point for about half a mile upstream, past the Pilchard canning factory, to the "Curtis and Pape" boat yard. With the trawl aboard and an extra pair of oars in the Hilda for Shirley to use, on the first of an early afternoon flood tide Shirley and I rowed to Trenant Point. I shot the trawl over the transom whilst Shirley rowed Hilda. As soon as I had belayed the 10-fathom towing warp to the aft ring bolt, I rowed with the second pair of oars. With the flood tide behind us and both of us rowing hard, the Hilda surged up the river. I remember thinking as we passed the canning factory that I had `cracked it`. I believed we were moving fast enough for the trawl to `fish` properly. When we drew abreast the boatyard, I decided to haul and see what we had caught. I shipped my oars and told Shirley to `backwater` her oars. This took the way off Hilda, and in no time, I had the trawl up and over the transom. The bag seemed pitifully small compared to the huge bags of sand and seaweed I had previously toiled with. I slipped the `cod end` knot and shook the contents on the stern `sheets`. What fell out was almost `clean` fish with just a few small `nubs` of seaweed and some stones. Shirley and I made `joyful noises`. We picked up the flapping` fish and put some of them in our box; about three-quarters of the catch were very small fish, which we took great care in returning to the river while they were still alive. I have a clear recollection of taking stock of our first haul, of being absolutely amazed at the different species. I had only expected to catch flounders and perhaps the odd bass, grey mullet or silver eel. In all probability, the different species of fish which frequented that part of the river were attracted there by the offal dumped in the river from the canning factory. All of the fish we had saved was just the minimum landing size. There were no large fish; it was as if we had trawled through a fish nursery. We had a few of each species of flounders, plaice, three brills, a turbot and three dover soles.

We rowed back to Trenant Point and shot the trawl once more. This time the flood tide was flowing faster, the Hilda seemed to glide effortlessly over the water pulling the trawl, and we reached the boatyard much quicker than the first tow. I hauled the trawl once more, but this time the bag was smaller than the first haul. We were disappointed. When I slipped the bag, we had caught less under size fish, but almost the same amount of fish large enough to keep. I can`t recall the number of species from the second haul, but we had two decent size bass. We were both `on a high`. We had drifted farther upstream; the return journey to Trenant Point against the tide took a lot longer to row than before. The tide was now in full spate, so with much regret, I decided to call it a day. We had achieved two successful hauls. Shirley and I were elated. We rowed the Hilda back to her mooring on `little beach` without a care in the world, discussing the next time we would trawl the west river. We divided the fish between us and went home. My father was at sea, and my mother was at work, so I shared all my fish with our next-door neighbours. Mrs Hocking, Mrs Wickett, who were pensioners, Gran` Soady and my aunt Maud. The reckoning came, for me, the next day. The guy who lived in Trenant Point house had seen us trawling and reported me to Arthur Hosking, the Harbour Master. I was giving a severe `tongue lashing` and a reprimand for trawling in the river with the threat that if I did it again without his say so, I would have my waterman`s licence revoked. The comical part of this encounter was after my admonishment. He asked me if we had caught any fish, and we ended up having a deep discussion centred on the various species of fish we had caught up by the canning factory. Shirley and I were never to trawl the west river or yet join forces aboard the Hilda again. The trawl was stowed away in the store. I realised that a boat with an engine was the tool needed to work the trawl properly. Two years were to pass until the summer of 1954 before the beam trawl was to see the light of day again.

Chapter 6: Nina Janet Chapman

1953 was a definitive year. In April, I severely injured my right knee playing football for the Liskeard Grammar School first XI, and I spent much of my recuperative time each day sitting in the shelter on Looe Seafront. I hardly saw anyone from day today, and it was refreshing when, one day, a pretty young woman; who was pushing a baby in a pram, stopped and we struck up a conversation. For the next few days, she returned, and I learned that her name was Nina Chapman; she also revealed that the baby was not hers, but he was Peter, her young half-brother. She had recently moved to Looe with her parents from Newport, Gloucestershire `en route` to Canada and at that time, they were residing at `Whitegate`, a large house on Hanafore Road, West Looe. Nina was exactly nine months to the day, my junior. We started to go out together, and almost six years later, we were married.

Although Nina was a `landlubber` from Gloucester and had never been aboard a boat before, she took to being on the water like the proverbial duck, and when I had healed from my injury, for that summer, we spent a lot of time together on the Hilda. Nina was a quick `learner` and was soon proficient in rowing. No matter what time of the evening or morning I wanted to go to sea, sometimes at daybreak, she would turn up and be beside me as my crew.

As a landlubber, unlike me, she did not suffer from sea sickness; the only thing that spooked her were spider crabs (Skerries). Each time a Skerry came up in a pot, I had to return it to the sea "tout suite" to stop Nina freaking out. One favourite trip was to row to the upper reaches of the west river and have a picnic at Shallow Pool. I remember the peace and tranquillity, the trout lying stock still, stemming the flow of fresh, translucent water, a silver flash breaking the surface to gulp at a fly. Espying a kingfisher perched on an overhanging bough; or a lone Heron, statuesque, patiently waiting for the next meal to swim past. A pair of swans with their five cygnet offspring trailing along behind as they glided gracefully downstream. It was an idyllic period for us when time just seemed to stand still.

One event that I will never forget was having a boat race with Jack Yeo, an old ferryman who was once a crewman with my father. He owned a 16ft rowing and sailing boat named "Bluebird". We had met up with Jack at Shallow Pool a couple of times when he had carried visitors to see the beautiful spot. I can`t remember how our conversation went, except I ended up having a 6d bet that I could beat him in a race from Looe bridge to Shallow Pool on the first of a flood tide. Being tidal, on the low water, the West River is no more than a small stream of fresh water meandering down the valley through mud flats to join up with the east Looe tributary at Trenant Point and from there to the open sea.

Going up the river on the first of the flood tide, there was no way Blue Bird could beat the Hilda with her much shallower draft. I thought this was money for old rope. After lunch on race day, both boats were moored below the Looe Bridge. Jack had paying passengers on board the Bluebird; there was only Nina and me aboard the Hilda. With all that weight in his boat, we had a distinct advantage. As the tide came in, the Hilda came afloat before the `Bluebird` and using the boat hook. I poled her upstream. Our passage up the west river was going well. We were past Heron`s Grove on our starboard hand, past the canning factory and the Curtis and Pape boat yard to port, well ahead of the Blue Bird. At times Hilda`s keel would touch bottom, and a few times, we were stuck in the channel until she lifted off on the surge of the flood tide. Occasionally we could see the Blue Bird astern of us and lose sight of him again when we rounded the next bend in the river. With the flood tide running faster, Blue Bird seemed to be gaining on us. Then disaster struck. I was too preoccupied looking astern and not concentrating on navigating the narrow channel when the boat hook got stuck in the mud, I lost my grip on it, and the Hilda drifted on with the boat hook left behind in the mud. By the time I had slipped the lashing off the oars, the Hilda was out of control and ended up stuck on the bank broadside across the tide. To our dismay, by the time the Hilda had refloated, and I had regained control, Jack Yeo had squeezed Bluebird past us in the narrow channel, laughing and hurling verbal abuse about my seamanship. My pride was hurt, try as I may, with the tide in full flood, I could not pass Bluebird again. When we eventually arrived at Shallow Pool, I paid Jack the 6d with bad grace, knowing I would be the laughing stock of the ferrymen fraternity in the weeks to come. I was always a bad loser, no matter what the competition. Winning was all that mattered!

Jack Yeo

The idyllic summer of 1953 came to a close, a fantastic time which Nina and I would not have experienced had Hilda not conveyed us everywhere. Little did I realise at that time in early September 1953, when the Hilda was hoisted up to her rafters berth in my fathers` store at the Albatross that our partnership was never to be renewed again.

Whilst writing about Hilda and my friendship with Steve Cox, I can recall two laughable incidents in which Steve was involved

The first incident I remember involving Steve happened on a winters` day during the pilchard season in the early 1950s. An uncle of mine, Robert (Bobby) Sargent, was a temporary crew for Steve in his small boat. I think she was called `Florence May`. One might say that my uncle Bob and work were `aliens`, much of the money he earned was swiftly deposited in any local hostelry for *`the devil's brew`* (*My great grandfathers` term for any alcoholic beverage. He was a Methodist Lay preacher*).

Bobby Sargent

That winter, pilchard shoals were close inshore and immense; every boat that could carry a pilchard net left harbour after lunchtime each day hoping to have a share of the silver harvest. The boats would return just after dark, tie up and pick the pilchards out of the nets. The local term for this was "shaking out". With a large catch, 'shaking out,` the fish could last all night. I have experienced `shaking out` all night many times. This particular evening the Florence May returned to the harbour with a big catch of pilchards, which had to be `shaken out`. According to my uncle, after the boat was berthed, Steve had remarked that if my uncle Bob had not been there, the money received when the fish was sold would all be his (Steve`s) own. The result was Uncle Bob took off his oilskin smock, climbed the ladder onto the quayside, turned to Steve and said that if that was the way Steve felt, he (Steve) could have the lot and then proceeded to the nearest pub, which happened to be the Salutation Inn. Steve was left with a boatload of Pilchards still in the nets and had to wait until the next morning to pay a scratch crew "*over the odds*" to help `shake out` and land the pilchards.

There has to be a moral with regard to greed somewhere in that story!!

Steve and I would often chat and compare lobster catches after our boats were moored up. This particular day, Steve had put his boat on the lifeboat slipway because she was leaking badly; he had clipped a rock whilst hauling his pots. I offered to help. While we were waiting for the tide to recede so we could repair the leak, there was an unbelievable foul smell wafting from the boat. I asked him if he could smell it; he said I was not to worry. He thought it was only the bilge that needed scrubbing. The smell was so nauseating that I didn`t think it was coming up from the bilge; it had to be coming from something else. I said that I would search inside. I climbed aboard and began searching the bilge below the bottom boards. Other than bilge slime and a florin, the bilge was clear. The boat had a forward locker, like most boats of that size for stowing fishing gear etc. The smell was definitely coming from the locker, which I opened up and the stench that came forth was overpowering. I wretched as I removed a small fish box covered with an oilskin apron. Beneath the apron were three large lobsters in the initial stages of decay. "*Ah!*" said Steve, "*There they are. I wondered what had happened to them. I knew I`d put them somewhere.*"

Apparently, a local hotel had placed an order with Steve for three large lobsters on Saturday. *This day was a Monday, nine days after Steve had received the order!*

Sadly, Hilda and I had sailed our last voyage together, and now, almost 70 years later, all I have are my memories of our six summers' partnership and one old creased photograph.

The Hilda remained lashed to the rafters in the Albatross store for the next four years, as she was for the years in the 1930s and 1940s leading up to my tenth birthday, until purchased by my cousin Joyce and her husband Tom Dix on the 26 June 1957.

Chapter 7: A New Boat

During the summer of 1953, it was rumoured that my friend Edward Toms was getting a motor boat named Dunlin to replace his rowing boat Pixie. The rumour was that his elderly grandfather Walter 'Watt' Toms (pronounced like 'rat') was going to buy the boat for Edward. I guess at that time. I was envious; I used to dream of what I could do if I had a boat with an engine.

It was 1954; I was 16 years old and in the sixth form at Liskeard Grammar School purely because my parents would not allow me to be a fisherman. I had no inclination to leave school and do what they wanted me to do, which was to get a 'proper job'. My mind never wavered from me being a fisherman. However, as this was my final year, I was told that I had to make up my mind to do `something`. Eventually, I had an interview with a careers officer, stemming from which I took the Devonport Dockyard Apprenticeship exam and, although I put very little effort into it, I passed it. There were multiple vacancies for electricians, shipwrights, blacksmiths and engine fitters; none of which interested me, so I chose the sole vacancy for a Torpedo Electrical Fitter Apprenticeship. I chose this because I thought it must be good as it was the only vacancy for that kind of job. The education attached to the five-year apprenticeship included the first four years at Devonport

Engineering College. My apprenticeship was not due to start until 6 September 1954, so I was looking forward to another summer fishing with the *Hilda*, but then fate took a hand.

Gone were the days of taking the train to Liskeard and home again from school. The train had been replaced by a school coach. At least we didn't have to walk the mile from Liskeard Station to school and back each day because the bus dropped pupils off outside school. I would normally leave the coach at the East Looe end of the bridge and walk home through the town, but on this particular day, in February 1954, I chose to go along the quay. As I passed Arthur Collings' boat building yard, I noticed the lights were on and heard work still being carried out. Curiosity got the better of me, so I opened the small personnel door situated in the main large double doors and ducked my head, though. When inside, I could see Mr Collings was working on a small boat that looked lost in the vast space of the building.

"Hello," he said, *"what do*'ee *want 'ere, boy?"* I said that I had seen the lights on and wanted to know what was being built. The boat he was working on was the epitome of the kind of boat I wanted. Longer than my *Hilda*, it was a couple of planks higher and had a larger beam. Mr Collings, in answer to my question, said that the boat was 16feet long and was for Bill Hocking, a fisherman who lived in Downderry (a village along the coast about three miles to the east of Looe). Bill wanted the boat to work off Downderry

beach for crab potting. I asked how soon the boat would be completed. He answered, *"About another two weeks."*

Bill Hocking aboard the "Neptunes Pride", the twin to the "Seahorse"

I was mesmerised; there and then, I knew I had to have a boat like this. Nervously, I asked how much an identical boat to the one on the stocks would cost to build. He responded, *"Come into the office, boy."* The office was a cubicle about the size of a red telephone box and tucked away in the corner of the yard. We squeezed into the office, and, after shuffling through some papers, Mr Collings licked a pencil stub and began to scribble on a piece of paper. *"Same size as this one, eh? Larch plankin' an' oak timbers, copper rivets that`ll be the boat. Bottom boards, stern name board, for'rd locker, a mizzen, mizzen mast and outrigger, pair of paddles and rowlocks, boathook and engine box. Three coats of paint or* *varnish and the bottom anti-fouled. What colour mizzen wud 'ee like, red or grey?" "Red, please," I chose. "Do 'ee 'av an engine?" I answered, "No." "Well," he said, "you'll 'av to supply th` engine, propeller an' shaft, stern tube an' bearing, petrol tank an' petrol, fuel an' water pipes an' sea cock, an' we'll fit 'em all. That'll cost 'ee a hundred an' twenty pounds. We've got a thirty-footer to build next,* so *if 'ee wants one like this, 'ee 'av to put yer order in soon so we can fit 'ee in and 'ee 'av to let us 'av a ten-pound deposit."*

Petrol rationing was abolished around 1950, but Mr Collings still expected the purchaser to supply their own petrol. I thanked him, and after another lingering look at the boat that Bill eventually called "*Neptune's Pride*", my head was in a whirl as I walked home. The question uppermost in my mind: where could I lay my hands on a £120 in a hurry? At that time, £120 seemed a fortune to me.

My father was in from sea when we sat down for tea, which I recall was fried whiting again. My mother wasn't the greatest at fish filleting, so invariably, I always managed to get bones in my fish. I purposely waited until we had almost finished eating, then I mentioned that I had been inside Mr Collings' boatyard on the way home and what a great small boat he was building. My father commented that it was for 'Downderry Bill', the name Bill Hocking was known by Looe fishermen.

I remember thinking, *well, here goes, nothing ventured, nothing gained.* So I announced, *"Mr Collings said a new boat like that would only cost a hundred and twenty pounds."* Before I could say anything else, my mother was apoplectic. *"Only a hundred and twenty pounds!" she screeched. I was mesmerised by a vein that was throbbing on her temple. "Where do you think you are going to get that sort of money? A hundred and twenty pounds, d'you think me and your father are made of money? You can forget any new boat. There won't be time for messin' around in any boat when you go to college in Plymouth. I don't want to hear anything more about a new boat. Well, say something, Fernley."* Her last remark was directed at my father, who muttered something along the lines of, "*Tis a lot of money."* Obviously, he did not want to get involved in my mother's verbal onslaught towards me. I realised that my strategy had failed miserably, so I thought it best to keep quiet. I remember, when I went to bed that evening, my head was full of different schemes to raise the money so I could place an order for the new boat. What I eventually decided, before I drifted off to sleep, was that my father was the 'Achilles heel'. I would tackle him about financing the new boat for me at the first opportunity when my mother was not around.............!

Mid-morning on Saturday, 13 February 1954, I found my father aboard the Endeavour mending a net. I stood back out of his sight in the fish market rehearsing my plea for the money, and then I climbed aboard to ask my father if he had seen the boat in Collings' yard and whether he thought she was worth the cost. My father previously had two boats built by Arthur Collings. By asking if he thought the boat was worth the money, I hoped he would engage in dialogue about money. Yes, he had seen the boat and thought the price was about right for a 16-footer. No more beating around the bush.

"Dad, will you lend me the money for a new boat like Downderry Bill's? I need to know soon because Mr Collings has a 30-footer to build, but if I put in an order right away, he will build one for me next."

He stopped mending and asked how I would repay him. I said that with a larger boat than the Hilda with an engine, I could work double the amount of pots and go long lining and trawling. I had about two months in the summer before I went to lodge in Plymouth for college and was sure I could earn enough money to pay him back. I still have this vivid memory of him tuning his back on me as he resumed mending the net — my heart sank. But without turning around again, he simply said, *"Okay, but don't tell yer mother."*

I was bursting with anticipation. Thanking him profusely, I promised to pay him back before the summer was over. I scrambled up the ladder to get to the boatyard as quick as I could to place the order for my new boat. The boat shed was closed. Utter dismay. Arthur Collings was an ardent supporter of Plymouth Argyle; of course, it was Saturday, and that afternoon the Argyle was playing at home to Leicester City.

Saturday afternoon seemed to drag on endlessly. I decided to go to Mr Collings' house in Higher Market Street later that evening, once he had arrived home from Plymouth, to order my boat. I arrived at his house and knocked on the front door. Mrs Collings greeted me, and I asked if I could speak to Mr Collings. She invited me in and called to her husband that there was 'a young gentleman' to see him. She ushered me into their sitting room. I thought how much warmer and cosier their house was compared to our two-up, two-down cottage in the back streets. Mr Collings was 'buried' in a huge armchair in front of a log fire. The scene was bizarre. He had a Mynah bird sitting on his shoulder, which had moulted and lost most of its plumage, who at random intervals squawked, "*Hello, Mother.*" I can't remember what it was called, but I couldn't help laughing at the scrawny, squawking bird.

I said that I would like to place an order for a boat, identical to the one he was building for Mr Hocking, and when could I sign the contract. He said, *"Us don't 'av contracts, boy, an 'and shake'll do."* He held out a gnarled hand, and we shook hands firmly. My order was placed, and I was over the moon. Mrs Collings showed me to the door, and as I was leaving, a voice called out, *"Dun ee fergit the ten-pound deposit, boy. 'Ee can bring it into us on Monday."*

When I went home that evening, I found it extremely difficult to contain this secret from my mother; I was brought up to '*always tell the truth and shame the Devil*'. Now, I was "lying by omission". I had a problem; I counted my money and had less than £5 in my name. I had told Nina that I was saving up for an engagement ring. As luck would have it, the next day, Sunday, we had poor weather, and my father was not at sea. When my mother went out to work after lunch, I told my father that I had ordered my boat and needed the £10 deposit by tomorrow, Monday. He calmed my anxiety, and I was not to worry; the weather forecast was bad for Monday, so he would pay the deposit as he would not be at sea. It was funny, but all day at school, I kept wondering if my father had paid it or if he'd forgotten. As soon as I jumped off the school bus, I headed straight for the boatyard. I ducked through the door, and before I could ask the question, Mr Collings said, *"Yer father's bin in an' paid yer deposit, so we'll start yer boat in a couple o' weeks' time*." I could hardly contain myself when I arrived home. Luckily, my mother was out to work, so I thanked my father, and all he said was, *"Don't ferget you'll have to pay me back and don't tell yer mother."* At that time, it never dawned on me that eventually, she would find out about my new boat, I was so pumped up with anticipation and excitement — the future was bright.

One other person who also gave me grief over my order for the new boat was my girlfriend, Nina. She was extremely unhappy because we had talked about getting engaged in the near future (although I was only 16 years old and she wouldn't be 16 until the following June), and the money I had saved was supposed to be for an engagement ring. I eventually placated Nina by saying she wouldn't have to row the *Hilda* anymore and '*we*' would earn a lot more money with a motor boat that would enable me to purchase the engagement ring a lot sooner. Luckily for me, the policy of appeasement worked, and life on that front ran smoothly again.

Mr Collings said that he hoped to begin building my boat by March 1st. All that day at school, it was as if I had ants in my pants. I could not settle, and Miss Yule, the art teacher, sent me out of class for failing to put a brush to canvas and daydreaming. The bus seemed to take an age to reach Looe. I recall getting off the bus and running to the boatyard. The boat had been started. The keel was laid, and Mr Collings was putting up the moulds around which the planking would be shaped. I watched in fascination until Mr Collings finished work for the day. I was in trouble again when I arrived home. Tea had started without me, and I was grilled by my mother about why I was so late getting home from school. Luckily, my father was at sea; the excuse I gave escapes me, but once again, I was not Mr Popular with my mother.

That evening, I waited on the pier until my father returned from pilchard drifting. I couldn't wait to tell him that the keel was laid for my new boat. As usual, the man of few words said something similar to, *"That's good, does your mother know?"* and carried on weighing the baskets of pilchards. I said that she didn't, to which he muttered something along the lines of, *"She'll find out sooner or later."* End of conversation.

I had a bigger problem than my mother finding out about the boat. I had no engine. With the boat being built, I wondered how much time I had to get an engine and all the attachments before Mr Collings would need to install them. I asked him, and he said that he planned to finish the boat by Easter. He wanted her out of the yard by then because he was going to start on the thirty-footer after Easter. He needed the engine by the end of March. Easter Sunday in 1954 was April 18th. I had four weeks to buy an engine from somewhere before it was needed, but the question was, from where? There was Martins Garage in East Looe with Jack Stanton and Bassett's Garage in West Looe. My enquiries at both garages for a small engine drew a blank. Time was running out for me to supply Arthur Collings with an engine, and I remember one particular day at school, in a history lesson, a feeling of absolute hopelessness swept over me. Richard III, at the Battle of Bosworth Field, was supposed to have cried, *"A horse, a horse! My kingdom for a horse!"* For me, I was crying inside, "*an engine, an engine! My kingdom for an engine!"*

Albert Daems

Two more weeks had flown by; the boat was taking shape, but still no engine. I was getting seriously worried. Mr Collings had enquired when the engine was going to arrive. No way could I afford a new engine. Then, once again, fate took a hand. Albert Daems, the World War II refugee Belgian fisherman, who was a crew with my father on the *Endeavour*, had a small ferry boat I think called the "*Linda"*. She was hauled up on the top of the lifeboat slipway for the winter and secured to the railings to survive the storms should the sea pound the seafront and slipway. I remember Albert saying that he was going to put the *"Linda"* up the river 'under the woods' because her planking and part of her keel had rotted in places, and he was thinking of getting another ferry boat for the summer. (Under the woods was the boats' graveyard in Looe) Albert's boat had a one-and-a-half-horsepower Stuart Turner petrol engine with a reverse gear. Only a few of the Stuart Turner engines of that size were fitted with a reverse gear. I remember thinking, "*I've got to have that engine, even if I have to buy the whole boat to get it.*"

Me by the "Linda" from where I got the engine for the "Seahorse"

The *Endeavour* was not at sea this particular day. I had to pass Albert's cottage on my way home from school. He lived five doors down the street from me on the other side, so I knocked on his door, and Mrs Daems invited me in. Without beating around the bush, I asked him if he would sell his old boat to me. He asked me why I wanted his old boat when I knew she was unseaworthy. I said I only wanted the engine and all the appurtenances. *"How much you give me?"* he asked. (Albert's English was not good.) I offered him £10 for the engine and all the bits. He wanted £50. We haggled for a while. Eventually, we agreed that Albert would sell me the engine and all the relevant parts for £25, with the understanding that I removed the engine and parts from the old boat. Albert also agreed to make a trawl to suit the new boat. At the time, it seemed a great deal for me, buying a Stuart Turner engine with reverse gear for only £25? Never mind the fact that I did not have £25! That `small detail` did not enter the equation at that very moment; the fact remained, I had an engine at last. Another hurdle had been overcome.

I had to wait until the Saturday after our deal to inspect Albert's boat and see what I'd bought. The truth finally dawned on me about the task ahead. I had to strip everything out of the boat. I had no tools and, more to the point had no clue how to dismantle the parts. Well, once again, nothing ventured, nothing gained, so when no one was aboard, I borrowed the tools I thought I might need from the toolbox on the *Endeavour*. I found that when I started dismantling the accessories and unbolting the engine, it was not as difficult as I anticipated. As my father's store in the Albatross building on the East Looe seafront was so close to the top of the lifeboat slipway, I put each part I dismantled in the store. The most difficult parts to remove were the propeller shaft and stern tube, but with Albert's help, I managed to finish taking out everything I wanted over two weekends and returned the Endeavour's tools without them being missed. I informed Mr Collings that I had an engine and all the accessories. Albert told my father that I had bought the engine from him, which prompted my father to ask how much I paid Albert for it and where had I got the money from. I said that I hadn't paid for the engine and didn't have the £25. I was hoping he would lend me the cash because it was the only engine available, and it was crucial I had it for the new boat before she was completed. My father was so good. He said that I'd better get the engine overhauled, and he would pay Albert, adding, *"Don't ferget you got to pay me back and don't tell yer mother."* When I think back, here was a man who did not want me anywhere near any fishing boat but to get a proper job, yet he financed a new boat for me with hardly a question.

As the engine had not been started since the previous summer, even I knew that it required a complete overhaul.

That was the next problem — who would overhaul it for me? Who could I ask? My next day at school was spent in a maelstrom of thoughts about how to get the engine sorted. Walking home from the school bus one evening, I saw the light on in the marine workshop. How could I forget that Ken Newton had set up a marine engineering workshop? Probably because it was hidden behind the fishermen's stores. I went into the workshop to tell Ken that I had Albert's Stuart Turner engine from his old boat and ask if he could help me. (His son Robert was to be my eldest son-in-law 24 years later.) I can only say that Ken Newton could not do enough to help in servicing the engine. I transported the engine and all the other parts from the Albatross store to the workshop on my father's net wheelbarrow. For the next two weeks, I spent all my spare moments working on the engine under Ken's tuition. He provided the handbook, all the necessary tools for me to strip down the engine, all the spares necessary (new piston and rings, etc.) to replace worn parts and the Stuart Turner green engine paint to finish the job. He helped me straighten the blades of the propeller and checked my reconstruction work on the petrol and water pipes, petrol tank and propeller shaft. The proof was in the pudding when the day came to bench test the engine. It burst into life at my second swing of the starting handle — there was no electric start. We didn't do high-fives in the 1950s, but a strong handshake from Ken and a *"well done, lad"* from him was praise indeed. At the age of 16, I could now strip down and rebuild an engine and, thanks to Ken, troubleshoot if things went wrong, which they invariably did from time to time with that model of a temperamental petrol engine. For all the help Ken had been, he would never take a penny piece for helping me, so I said that he would have the first cock crab I caught from the new boat. In fact, it transpired later that I was happy to drop a crab into the workshop from time to time. I took the engine to Mr Collings just in time. He was at the stage of the build to install the engine.

With all the time I was spending out of our home, my mother was beginning to get suspicious. Her questions about where I was and what had I been up to were more than her normal nosiness. Naively, I was still under the illusion that I could carry on without her finding out about the new boat. That naive `bubble` was soon about to burst! After a normal day at school, I arrived home and sat down to the usual fare of fried fish, bread and butter, and a cup of tea. The four of us sat were around the table when the wrath of hell descended upon me once again in the form of my mother. I'm afraid I have no true recollection of my mother's fury, except that I was shocked and caught off-guard. She had, somehow or other, discovered I was having a new boat built. My only memory is that the tirade carried on for so long that finally, my father intervened and, in an uncharacteristic manner, raised his voice to say, *"That's enough. I gave him the money."* An eerie quiet descended on the room as my mother rose and left the table without another word. In retrospect, at that moment, there was no doubt who wore the trousers in our home. The next few days were accompanied by a chilled wind blowing through the house; you could have cut the air with a knife. In hindsight, I was foolish and should not have tried to deceive my mother, and I should have involved her in the project much sooner. Once again, my father had bailed me out.

I eventually brought my mother round and placated her by offering an olive branch and took her to see how the boat was progressing. I was so chuffed when I heard Mr Collings tell her that she should be proud of what I had achieved at my age in having a new boat built. Following that visit, my relationship with my mother became much closer. I am sure I had Arthur Collings to thank for helping peace to reign again at home.

Chapter 8: The Seahorse

Mr Collings asked me what I was going to name the boat because he had to put her on the boat register and carve the name on her backboard. I discussed this with Nina. After mulling over many names and because the engagement ring was far on the horizon, I allowed her to choose the name '**Seahorse**'. *Seahorse* was good for me. With the Easter school holiday imminent, it was all systems go to prepare the *Seahorse* for launch on Easter Monday. My dream was finally a reality. The *Seahorse* was painted in gleaming white inboard and out, anti-fouled red on the bottom with varnished gunwales, thwarts, engine box, oars, boathook, mizzen mast and outrigger. The name "**Seahorse**" was carved into the backboard and picked out with white gloss paint to stand out against the varnished background.

Easter Monday dawned with dry weather and a moderate northwest wind blowing out the river. In the morning, just Nina and I met at the boat shed where the *Seahorse* was lifted onto a trolley and conveyed over the quay to the lifeboat slipway. No breaking a champagne bottle over the bow, Nina and I just climbed aboard, and the *Seahorse* was unceremoniously launched into the harbour by Arthur Collings. I hitched her to a quayside ladder, just to the north of the slipway, and checked for any leaks. She was sound and tight, a tribute to the skill of Arthur Collings. He looked over the edge of the quay and asked if there were any leaks. I said she was fine, and without further ado, he said, *"She's all yours now, me sonny, good luck,"* before strolling nonchalantly back up the quay. To this day, I remember being speechless. He had fulfilled my dream, yet it appeared to him that it was just another day at the office!

I opened the seacock, and the engine spluttered into life after a couple of swings of the starting handle. I looked over the port side and, after what seemed like an eternity, the cooling water spurted out from the exhaust water pipe. Everything seemed fine. As a final check, although we were still hitched to the ladder, I let the engine tick over for a while and then put the lever in forward gear. I expected propeller wash to come from astern, but nothing happened. The *Seahorse* didn't move forward an inch. I lifted off the propeller shaft guard tunnel and saw that the shaft wasn't turning. I shifted the gear lever from forward through neutral to reverse, but there was still no movement with the shaft, so I put the lever in neutral. Nina asked what was wrong, and I pointed out that the shaft was not turning with the engine in gear. I went through the same motions again, but there was no shaft movement. I was at a loss as to what the trouble was. I decided to moor the *Seahorse* where she was and seek out Ken Newton. Both Nina and I were deflated, devastated; we could not believe how one minute we were on the crest of a wave and, in such a short while, had hit rock bottom. It was

Easter Monday. I had no idea where Ken would be, so Nina and I decided to go for a walk to Hannafore, a district of West Looe, where Ken lived. There was more disappointment to come because he wasn't home.

The next day, I checked that the *Seahorse* was okay and was waiting at the engineering workshop when Ken arrived to open up. I explained what had happened. He grabbed his tool bag and said, *"Let's go and have a look."* Ken started the engine and tried the gear lever first forward, then in reverse a couple of times and finally stopped the engine. He uncoupled the shaft from the centrifugal clutch and dismantled the clutch cover. I can't remember exactly what he said next, only that it was peppered with expletives, interspersed with words like 'stupid', 'idiot' and 'moron'—all seemingly directed at me. He was grinning at the same time. He asked me for a clean rag. He wiped the inside of the clutch cover and reassembled the clutch and propeller shaft. *"Right,"* he said, *"start her up and put her in gear."* I started the engine, put it in forward gear, and the *Seahorse* leapt ahead, straining on the stern mooring rope. *"Okay, that's enough, knock her out."* I obeyed the order, and the *Seahorse* relaxed to swing back on the bow rope. I still couldn't understand what had been wrong. He laughed again and said, "*You did too good a job with the grease. You should never put grease on the inside of a centrifugal clutch cover. The grease was stopping the Ferodo clutch linings from gripping the casing. That's why the propeller wouldn't turn. Let's take her out on her maiden voyage."* During the time Ken had been working, Nina had arrived, so I slipped the ropes, jumped back aboard and proudly, at last, spun the *Seahorse* around in the middle of the river and motored past the Banjo Pier out to sea. It was to be the first of many trips.

Chapter 9: Cricket

There was still about three months of school term left before the summer holiday and the end of my grammar school era. As I had passed the apprenticeship exam, the teachers weren't bothered if I attended their lessons or not. I finished off the football season playing for the School First Eleven and then played for the School First Eleven Cricket Team at the commencement of the cricket season. Running down the days of the summer term in the sixth form until my time was over with Liskeard Grammar School, I again played for the school cricket team. Herein lay a problem for me; the home matches were played in the evenings and finished after the last bus and train had left Liskeard for Looe. Finally, that problem was solved for me when I had an offer of the loan of a bicycle so that I could ride home after the cricket match finished. The other part of this story is that I had never sat on or rode a bike in my life. My parents refused to let me have a bike because they said that it was unnecessary there were too many hills in Cornwall and that I could walk, catch a bus or train. I must say that my parents were right about the hills in Cornwall; I found that when riding a bicycle, the hills were much steeper going up than when going down.

The school day was over, and I was introduced to my `conveyance`. The bike was a drop handlebar, high saddle three-speed racing machine, on which I mounted with great trepidation. I can`t recall who steadied the bike for me while I got on, and the next thing I recall was hurtling along "Old Road", past the school buildings and towards the crest of "Coombe Hill", finally losing my balance and ending up on the wide grass verge and in the hedge with the bike on top of me. Someone laughingly suggested that I should have used the brakes! Hmm...How do I do that? I cannot remember who helped me out of the hedge, and from then on, the rest of that day is somewhat blurred. I know that I played in the cricket match against Callington Grammar School (I think), then rode home to Looe. I have vague recollections of falling off on the way down Coombe Hill, somewhere in Trewidland and at least another half a dozen times before I reached Lower Chapel Street. I managed to perfect a move that when I felt I was losing my balance, I decanted into the hedge for a "soft" landing. I arrived home mainly "by guess and by God!" and I remember feeling quite jubilant that I had managed to cycle uninjured, from Liskeard to Looe, but my mother was far from amused. As usual, she was unimpressed with my feat and `wittered` on about me using someone else` bike when I didn`t know how to ride.

The next morning I put the bike in the Guard`s Van and rode the train to Liskeard, cycling from Liskeard station to school instead of the usual bus ride from Looe. I`m not sure how many home cricket matches that I was involved in, but each time I travelled home on the bike, I never managed to arrive at our house without the usual mishaps on the way, each time returning on the train and riding the bike back to school. I have never ridden a bike since that time as I decided that I had some form of an impediment in my balance lobe! The sad part of this story is that I cannot recollect which friend had loaned the bike to me. I took full advantage of the teacher's blasé attitude towards me and spent the odd day off school preparing fishing gear for the *Seahorse*.

I have to add that during my Army National Service, I was "ordered" to learn to ride an Army motorcycle. Suffice it to say that after I had fallen off the machine three times, it finally dawned on the Sergeant in charge that I had no balance and to save the machine from being a complete "write off", he ordered me to learn to drive a two-ton Army lorry instead! I passed my driving test within five days!

Chapter 10: Fishing Gear for the `Seahorse`

My first lobster from the "Seahorse"

Try as I may, I have no recollection of my last day at Liskeard Grammar School, although my leaving certificate, signed by the headmaster Mr Lingard, is dated Tuesday, 27 July 1954. By the end of term, I had the *Seahorse* well-equipped with 700 hooks of long line. Much of this gear I had begged and scrounged from my father and two of my uncles, who were also fishing boat owners. Long lining is a passive method of fishing where baited hooks on three-foot strops are attached to a stout 'back' line at intervals of six feet. These are laid along the seabed in the hope of catching various species of fish: mainly bottom dwellers such as skate, ray, conger, turbot, whiting, dogfish, etc. For stowage, the lines are coiled down into a basket with the hooks embedded in a cork that surrounds the top of the basket. I had made up seven baskets of 100 hooks. When joined together, the long line stretched for 1400 yards along the seabed. Later in the summer, I found I could comfortably stow five baskets aboard the *Seahorse*, bait all 500 hooks, shoot the line and haul it single-handed.

Albert Daems made me a small trawl out of an old herring drift net, five fathoms on the footrope, just the optimum size for the *Seahorse* to tow. Those fishing methods were peripheral to and worked in tandem with my favourite pastime of crab and lobster potting. The pots, which remained from the preceding six summers on the *Hilda* (well, what was left of them), were in a poor state. I calculated that I could work 48 pots from the *Seahorse*, double the number I operated from the *Hilda*, in six strings of eight pots to a string. I also worked out that with reasonable weather and decent catches of crabs and lobsters, I could earn enough money to repay my father. The question was, where was I going to get that amount of new or decent second-hand pots from? Time was marching on. My time at grammar school was drawing to a close. I had accumulated all the back ropes, pot strops, Dhans and Dhan lines, but only a few decent pots. My father always said, *"Better an unlucky fisherman was never born!"* Well, I always thought that if that was true, I had best make my own luck.

L-R: Arthur Collings (boat builder), Harry Hocking (fish salesman), (unknown)

Harry Hocking Fisheries

Mr Harry Hocking, a major fish buyer in Looe, was on the board of the Looe Harbour Commissioners, as was my father at that time. Apparently, in the course of the conversation, my father had mentioned my new boat to Mr Hocking, which led to him (Mr Hocking) to offer me a deal. He had just opened "Harry`s Cockle Bar" on East Looe Quay where, as well as cockles, he sold whole crabs, crab meat and lobsters. At that time, Mr Hocking was in partnership with Mr Harry Worden in the construction of a new fishing boat by Arthur Collings; hence he no longer had a requirement for his crab pots as the intention for the new build was to go drift netting for pilchards. The deal was that I could have the pick of Mr Hockings` fleet of crab pots that were in his store adjacent to the cockle bar. He said that I could have use of as many pots as I wanted in return for me landing all the shellfish I caught, wholly and solely, for his cockle bar. He would pay me fixed prices for my crabs and lobsters: 2d per lb for hen (bun) crabs, 10d per lb for cock crabs and 1s 9d per lb for lobsters (irrespective of size, lobsters weighing one pound were highly sought after by restaurants and made more money than the larger ones). 1s 9d seemed a very good average price for mixed lobsters, so I didn't have any second thoughts — this was a deal I could not turn down. The main thing about this deal was that it cast aside any worries I had regarding where I was going to sell my catch. I had a guaranteed priced market for all my shellfish, and Mr Hocking had a guaranteed supply. We shook hands on the deal, and he gave me a key to the store where the pots were kept. I now had access to as many crab pots as I wanted.

"Frenchman" Crab Pots

I didn't use the pots that I had worked from the *Hilda*; I took 48 pots from Mr Hocking's store. They were all 'Frenchman pots', which were made in 'barrel' form from three-foot soft wood laths and hoops with 10-inch 'necks' to allow entry of the shellfish. This type of pot was not as good for catching small lobsters compared to the traditional Cornish willow(`withy`) inkwell shaped pot, but they completely outfished the small-necked Cornish `withy` pot when it came to Cock crabs, large lobsters and spider crabs. The disadvantage of the Frenchmen was that in poor weather, they tended to roll around on the seabed and were more susceptible to damage than the `withy`. Anyway, I had my pots, and I had 48 on the top of the lifeboat slipway, in six strings of eight, ready to be shot by the time my final day at the grammar school arrived. Two large stones were lashed in each Frenchman to give the pot negative buoyancy so the pot would sink. Extra stones were put in each pot for the first time of shooting until the pot became waterlogged when the extra stones were removed. There were also two bait nails tied inside the neck to which the bait was attached. I made a pair of wooden 'otter' boards for use with the trawl that Albert had made, and I also made up a pair of 5-fathom bridles and 40-fathom Manila rope towing warps. The day after I left school, working all day and late into the evening, I had baited and shot all the 48 pots in 6 strings of 8 pots. I remember thinking, "*I hope the weather stays fine*", as I had set myself a stern task, having less than six weeks to earn the £145 I owed my father £145.00 in 1954, which is equivalent to £4,072.47 in 2021.

My apprenticeship was due to begin on Monday, 6 September 1954. I had to be at my lodgings, which had been arranged for me by Devonport Dockyard, on Sunday, 5 September 1954. The boarding house was in Keppel Street, Devonport. I cannot recollect the number of the house or the name of the landlady; I only remember that she was a wartime widow. I was to share one large bedroom with three other new apprentices: Colin Rowe from Penzance, David Bindon from Polperro and a fourth boy I can't recall.

August 1954, for me, is just a fantastic, distant memory. The *Seahorse* fulfilled all my hopes. The weather during the month was fine, and I hardly missed a day from working my crab pots. The daily catch of lobsters and crabs surpassed my expectations. When anyone asked if I was catching any lobsters, I frequently quoted my old fisherman friend Steve Cox's words: *"Yes, one with one claw!"*

It was a major advantage being able to land my catch to Mr Hocking daily; to give him his due, after we weighed the catch, he always paid me in cash there and then. The *Seahorse* had no lights, so I used a Tilley lamp and two hurricane lamps when I was at sea in the dark. I had a few evenings trawling in the bays to the east and west of Looe. These were successful considering all the gear was new, and it took a few drags (tows) to get the trawl balanced with the trawl (otter) boards I had made.

Nina came with me the few times she wasn't required to help in her parents' guest house. Mr Hocking, once again, gave me the market price for all my trawl fish. My Uncle Leonard aboard his boat *Renee* was the only trawler out of Looe landing to the fish market at that time, so my small landings of plaice, soles, rays, turbot and dabs were highly sought after by Mr Hocking. Uncle Leonard did a lot of night-time trawling in all the bays. There were many mornings, en route to my pots, when I stopped the *Renee* returning to the harbour to have a five-stone basket of fresh gurnards for bait — supposedly the best fresh bait for lobsters.

August was finished, and so was my short season with the *Seahorse*. My father said that I had to put her in the store for the winter before I went to lodge in Plymouth on September 6th. I brought all the pots in during the first week in September and stowed them away in Mr Hocking's store. He said that if I wanted, we could repeat the arrangement next year. I said I would if I had the time; by going to live in Plymouth, I did not know what the future held for me.

We had our last trip around Looe Bay. During the Friday/Saturday, I put the *Seahorse* on the lifeboat slipway, stripped out all the gear and gave her a good scrub out. I intended to take out and overhaul the engine if I had any spare time during the winter months. With the help of a few hands that were thereabouts, the *Seahorse* was put in the store to keep company with the *Hilda*, which sadly had been "store bound" for all the summer of 1954.

Chapter 11: Payback Time and a Move to Plymouth

Saturday evening, 4 September 1954, I helped my father land his catch of pilchards. I have a clear memory of that evening because the boats rarely went to sea on Saturdays` and also, the *Endeavour*'s catch weighed exactly 100 stone. I remember my father saying that they might just as well have caught 99 stone and when I asked why, he explained that the buyer, Cornish Products, deducted two stone off the first 100 landed and another one stone for every 50 stone thereafter. So, although he had landed 100 stone, he would only be paid for 98 stone. The deduction was standard with all buyers because the pilchard is a very soft fish, and some would always get damaged whilst being shook out of the nets.

I waited until we had finished supper, then with a feeling of fulfilment and with a flourish, I presented my father with the £145 that he had loaned me all those months before. I think my mother was amazed — she just looked and never said a word; she just rose slowly from the table and started to clear the plates. My mother never spoke again about that money saga. The reason she remained silent I will never know to this day. I can only assume that she was so surprised I had eventually repaid my father and so quickly that she was rendered speechless! Contrary to my mothers` demeanour, my father said that I had done well to repay the money in such a short space of time. Praise indeed! But he emphasised that now was the time to forget all about fishing and to get my head into my books for the next five years so that I could get a "***proper***" job. Thinking back to that time and my father's fixation with a "***proper***" job, his words certainly fell on `stony ground`: I was never going to lose sight of my goal. I remember saying under my breath, "I will be a fisherman!"

With the *Seahorse* safely tucked away in the Albatross store; Sunday, 5 September 1954, came far too quickly for me; I had no inclination to be an apprentice or carry on with any college education in Plymouth. Very reluctantly, with my suitcase packed and after saying goodbye to my parents, I took the ferry across to West Looe and waited in the square with Nina for the 4:00 p.m. bus to Torpoint. I can still recall how miserable I felt. It was probably a combination of leaving home for the first time, no more fishing, being separated from Nina and the thought of living in a strange house with people that I didn`t know. I sat in the front seat upstairs on the double-decker bus. The journey to Torpoint seemed endless: traversing all the coastal villages through Seaton, Downderry, along the cliff road past Tregantle Fort and Whitsand Bay, eventually arriving at Torpoint. I caught the Torpoint Ferry across to Devonport and then took the number 8 bus (I think) to the top of Albert Road, Devonport, from where I walked to Keppel Street.

Much against my wishes, my five-year Electrical Torpedo Apprenticeship, allied to four years of engineering college, including night school, was about to begin. It was only five years later when I had finished the apprenticeship that I noticed the wrong age of 17, which had been written on my indentures. I was only 16 years of age at the start of my apprenticeship on 6 September 1954. Whilst lodging in Plymouth, I travelled home every other weekend on Friday evening, returning to Plymouth by bus to Torpoint ferry the following Sunday afternoon.

Chapter 12: The Skipper of Endeavour

Although this episode is nothing to do with my second boat, the *Seahorse*, this story fits in with the chronology during the early months of my life in Plymouth and was my first real insight into how hard it would be to earn a living as a full-time fisherman.

As usual, during the summer of 1954, the pilchard shoals in Cornish waters broke up, and, on the whole, this season for the driftnet fleet of Looe by any standards was very poor. By the end of September, my father decided to lay up his 35-foot fishing boat ***Endeavour (FY369)*** until, hopefully, the pilchards shoaled. November 5th was recognised by Looe and Polperro fishermen as the date that large shoals of pilchard usually arrived in local waters. Pilchard drifter crews were ageing and dwindling, and young replacements had become difficult to recruit. By the time the *Endeavour* returned to fishing on November 8th, my father's crew had consisted of Bob Brown, an engineer in his fifties, and Alfred Southern, a fisherman who I believe was well into his sixties (known as '*Leggy*').

I was home from Plymouth for the weekend on Friday, 12 November 1954. The large pilchard shoals were very flighty at this time. With all the Looe fleet engaged in pilchard drifting again, catches varied nightly from 200 stones for the top boat to no fish at all for many of the other boats. The *Endeavour* had landed half a ton (80 stones) of pilchards two days before on the previous Wednesday, 10 November 1954. The weather was bad on the following Thursday and Friday, so my father broke with tradition and went to sea on Saturday. Normally he and my mother would go to the Regent cinema on a Saturday evening where they had standing reservations for the 1s 9d seats one and two in row 'L' if my father was not at sea. When the *Endeavour* returned to harbour that Saturday evening, my father had to be helped ashore. He had hurt his back; obviously, Saturday the 13th was unlucky for him!

Bob Brown

Nina and I had used my parents' cinema tickets that evening, and when I arrived home, my father was flat on his back on a board in bed. Without `beating around the bush`, he asked if I would help crew the *Endeavour* the next day, Sunday. To say I was surprised was a massive understatement. My father had asked me, with no experience, to actually crew on the *Endeavour*. This was the father who, for years previously, had kept telling me to get a `proper job` and now actually wanted me to take his place on the boat! I agreed immediately without thinking. Looking back, it was a `rash` decision, considering my circumstances at that time....But, "Hey Ho!"...As far as I was concerned at that time, this was my `big` chance. It would mean that I would miss the Sunday afternoon bus back to Torpoint; anyway, I thought, what the hell… I could catch the early bus on Monday morning. I would probably miss reporting to the Torpedo Depot, but I would still be in time for an evening class at the Engineering College.

Sunday morning, I rang Nina (Looe 221) at Whitegate to tell her the news; suffice it to say that we exchanged `words`. She made her feelings quite clear and thought I was mad to miss returning to Plymouth on Sunday afternoon! Water off a duck`s back! After Sunday lunch, I quizzed my father on how many nets were aboard the *Endeavour* and where the boats were fishing. For the winter, the Endeavour carried a fleet of seven drift nets, each 60 fathoms (120 yards) long, 6 fathoms deep (36feet) `scunned` (tied) together to make a total length of approximately half a mile. He said that the pilchard shoals were in Mevagissey Bay the previous day, but his advice was to follow the *Valhalla*, owned and skippered by my father's elder brother, John (known as Jack). My mother packed some food for me, and off I went down to the quayside — into the unknown. I thought it funny at the time, but my mother made no comment on the situation. Looking back, perhaps it was more proof of who wore the trousers in the household. Anyway, this was my big moment.

With the *Endeavour* having a top speed of barely eight knots, it would take anything from an hour and a quarter to an hour and three-quarters, depending on the tidal flow, to steam to Mevagissey Bay from Looe. Bob Brown and Alfred Southern (Leggy) had already been contacted and told to be down at the harbour and ready for sea at 1:30 p.m. In 1950 my father had updated the original 30hp Lister main engine in the Endeavour and replaced it with a 36hp Swedish made `Bolinder` engine. (Ken Newton was the local agent for Bolinder`s) The 16hp Lister `wing engine` remained side by side with the `Bolinder` in the for'ard cabin. Bob had both engines running by the time I arrived on the quay, and smoke curled from the chimney on the foredeck as Leggy had lit the coal fire in the stove/oven situated in the cabin for'ard of both engines.

[‘Wing’ engine is the term used because the propeller of the 16hp Lister engine exited the hull under the port quarter of the boat and was used exclusively when retrieving the nets, which were hauled generally over the starboard rail so they would not foul the propeller.]

I climbed aboard, and Bob surprised me by saying, *“Okay, Skipper, all ready to let go.”* I said something like, *“Who me Bob? You not taking her?”*....... *“Nah! You’re the skipper, ain’t that right, Alf?”* Leggy nodded his head, *“Sure thing, Bob.”*

Thinking back, I wasn’t a bit nervous — I was too excited to be nervous. Today I was skipper of the *Endeavour* and my thoughts at that time were not to make a hash of swinging the *Endeavour* to leave the harbour. All boats at East Looe were always moored bow up the river, and they had a leg shipped against the port side so they would stay upright when grounding on the low water, so the Endeavour’s leg was unshipped and stowed, and mooring ropes slipped. I had the wheel; at that moment, I was in command, and the *Endeavour* was my complete responsibility. I can still remember the thrill of putting the `Bolinder` gear lever ahead and the wing engine astern — the *Endeavour* swung gracefully in her own length. Bow out the river, I put the wing engine from astern to ahead, and we were away, past the Riley`s Pier, Nailsea Rock. Open the full-throttle on both engines. Past the rusting mast of the mid-main rock marker on the starboard hand, concentrate on navigating the narrow channel between Looe Island to port and Hannafore to starb'd; past Dunker Rock to port, Horestone to starb'd, and we were away.........the *Endeavour* was bound to the west'ard for Mevagissey Bay. Bob and Leggy shipped the heavy mizzen outrigger, unshipped the net room boards and stowed them below in the for'ard fish room. The *Endeavour* was ready for action. I remember pondering the correct course to Mevagissey Bay. Was it west by south or west-southwest? I eventually settled the *Endeavour* on a course to follow the other Looe boats steaming westward.

The weather was overcast but fine, with only light southerly airs with a slight chill in the air. When we arrived, Mevagissey Bay was alive with boats of all sizes from Looe, Mevagissey, Polperro, Par, Charlestown, Gorran Haven and Falmouth. There were as many as 100 boats 'dodging' hither and thither, seeking a clear "berth" to shoot their nets. I noticed there was even a Plymouth drifter among us.

I knew what to look for, the signs of any pilchards: dark coloured water, oily water, storm petrels (known by fisherman as Mother Carey's chickens) dipping and skimming on the sea, a gannet diving from a great height. There were none of these tell-tale signs. It was getting late, and the winter light was beginning to fade (What the Looe fishermen called "dimpsy"). It was time the nets were in the water. All around us, boats were shooting their nets before the light wind. The *Valhalla* was close by and squaring away to shoot, so I said to Bob to get ready. Even today, almost 60 years later, I can still remember the excitement I felt making the decision to take a tight berth between the *Valhalla* and the Mevagissey Lugger *Snowdrop*. Each boat about 25 yards on either side of us.

I brought the *Endeavour* around before the wind, gave the order 'shoot away' and, without ceremony, Leggy tossed the "pole end" buoy overboard. After the first (pole end) net was in the water, a 10-foot Dhan with a hurricane lamp lashed to the top was attached to the nets and lowered into the water. (This light was to enable one to see where the end of the nets was after darkness fell.) The remaining six nets were shot; Bob and Leggy hoisted the mizzen. I shut down both engines, and the *Endeavour* came around to ride 'head to wind' and lay back on the taut "swing" rope. The "swing" rope was the rope connecting the end of the 'boat' net to a cleat on the foredeck.

With the engines quiet and cupping a mug of Leggy's hot tea in my hands, I remember vividly looking through the open wheelhouse window and soaking up the scene of a fleet of Cornish drifters riding, head to wind, to their nets in the gathering gloom. Uncle Jack's *Valhalla* to port and the *Snowdrop* to starb'd. The many different coloured "mizzen" sails, the drone of many voices filtered across the water. I remember getting a feeling of utter satisfaction when I could make out the yellow glow of our Dhan light flickering in the distance. The nets were still drifting in a fairly straight line, which would make hauling easier. This evening was a similar scene to one I had witnessed many times before, but only as a young passenger on the *Endeavour*. This time I was the skipper; I was in charge and had just turned seventeen years old. Riding lights, a red over a white light at the mastheads, were twinkling all around to warn shipping that fishing boats were 'out of control'. The soft sound of voices, a burst of laughter continued from across the water, and the smell of smoke from galley fires drifted on the light evening airs —this was what I had dreamt of for as long as I could remember. Such was bliss.

Darkness soon cloaked the fleet, and the masthead lights of the boats flickered over the calm water like fireflies, and after a while, an engine broke the silence. One skipper had decided it was time to haul his nets, and then another and another engine coughed into life. Deck lights flickered on throughout the fleet of boats and next on the *Valhalla*. My mind was made up: I decided it was our turn to "have a look-up". Leggy banked up the stove coal fire, we donned our oilskin smocks, and Bob started the wing engine. I switched on the single deck light and the light on an extended arm from the wheelhouse to shed light over the water on the starboard side where the nets were hauled. The starboard rail roller, the spar between the net room and the wheelhouse bulkheads were "shipped up". Leggy, as 'head rope' man, took his place on the aft side of the net room. Bob took up his berth as net stower behind me. We were ready.

From where I stood at the rail to haul the bottom of the net (the skirt), I had access to a long rod attached to the gear lever of the wing engine so I could 'go ahead' or 'astern' when required. This was my baptism at the rail. I recall putting the engine in gear and hauling in the swing rope with anticipation. Manually hauling the nets was so much harder than I had ever anticipated. My arms began to ache. I swear my arms had stretched inches longer by the time the half-mile of seven nets were hauled aboard. (I remember thinking at that time....now I know what a Gorilla feels like!)

Whilst we hauled, I kept looking around. The boats seemed to be getting their nets aboard in no time — all the signs of no fish. It was the same situation with us; very disappointing, just an occasional pilchard meshed by the gills, which a flock of screaming seagulls attracted by our lights were trying to steal. As I hauled, I noticed the air was getting damp, and slowly the visibility deteriorated. I was gradually losing sight of the other boat's lights, and finally, the lights of the *Valhalla* disappeared. The fisherman's worst enemy: thick fog. I must say, for a few moments, panic took over, but we still had some nets to get. I eventually got control of myself and concentrated on hauling the skirt as fast as I could. All thoughts of tired arms disappeared. With the Dhan light safely on board, the "pole end" net flew in over the starboard roller in double-quick time. The catch was just a few stones of pilchards; however, I felt relief that all the nets were safely back aboard, and in the fog, the *Endeavour* was free from the encumbrance of the nets, so I was able to manoeuvre in a hurry if absolutely necessary.

Fog horns started to wail from every direction. Panic again. What was the compass course back to Looe? (There was no such thing as satellite navigation at that time, just a compass and local knowledge and a watch, or in our case, an old alarm clock.) I switched out the deck and wheelhouse lights and peered into the fog — nothing to be seen. I had never experienced being caught in fog before without my father on board the *Endeavour*. I suggested to Leggy that he take the wheel as he had spent a lifetime of experience on the sea and once had owned his own "Lugger". He shook his head. *"Nah, boy, you'm skipper aboard 'ere!"* I turned to Bob and received the same answer before I even had a chance to pose the question to him. They seemed to have faith in me, or could it be that neither of them knew the course to Looe? I would never know. I put on a brave face and did not ask them if they knew what the course was to get us home; neither did I let them know that I wasn't sure of the course either. I remember being acutely aware of the responsibility shouldered by the skipper of any fishing boat compared to the carefree crewman. It was my responsibility to get Bob, Leggy, the *Endeavour*, not to mention myself, back safely to Looe.

I told Bob to stop the wing engine and switch on the deck lights again. At least I thought the *Endeavour* would be visible at close quarters. Without the thump of the diesel engine, we lay motionless, listening to the sounds surrounding us — a cacophony of engine noise coming from all directions. Bob cupped his hands to his ears and said that by the sound of one engine, the closest boat to us was still hauling its nets. I asked Leggy to make some tea and said, "*We'll lay for a bit with the engines stopped, have a `cuppa` and wait for most of the other boats to leave.*" I was in no rush to start back in this thick fog and was still pondering, in my mind, what was the course for Looe. With the engines stopped, we could hear what was happening to the boats which were still close to us. I was just hoping that the fog might lift. Leggy offered me the foghorn. I still laugh about it now. The foghorn was no more than a copper horn which one had to blow into like a bugle. I gave it a few blows, which was a complete waste of my breath. A serious-looking Leggy said, "*That thing is as useful as a glass eye to a blind man in a fog.*"

I can't recall how long we lay listening to the ever-decreasing engine sounds as more boats got under way for their home port. I remember sipping a mug of tea for so long that the dregs were cold — this made up my mind. It was time for us to get underway for home. The boat closest to us had finished hauling because the engine note changed, and the *Endeavour* rolled with the wash as she passed close to us. I remember taking a compass bearing. It could have been the *Snowdrop* bound for Mevagissey. After a while, I was satisfied that we were probably the last boat in the area. No engine sounds close to us, and the ones we could hear were gradually receding.

I gave Bob a hand to crank the starting handles, and both engines coughed into life. I turned off the lights except for the steaming light to the masthead, which cast an eerie yellow glow, and the red (port) and green (starboard) navigation lights on either side of the wheelhouse. I asked Leggy to light the hurricane lamp, which was on the Dhan, and lash it to the aft side of the mizzen mast to act as a stern light.

I put both engines in forward gear. I remember still thinking, *is the course to Looe east by north or east-northeast?* I plumped for the east by north, which I calculated was the safest course and would take us to the south'ard of Looe Island if the fog remained. Once we were past the island, we could stop and listen for the Looe fog horn. I spun the wheel until the compass card swung to where I hoped that the *Endeavour* was on the right course for Looe. I checked the blue alarm clock pocked with rust, which was fixed to the starboard side of the wheelhouse with a combination of nails and a piece of twine. I will never forget the time; it was 7:25 p.m. I calculated that we should be abreast of Looe Island in an hour and a half with an ebb tide against us. I set the alarm for 9:00 p.m.

Leggy came in the wheelhouse to tell me, sheepishly, that in attempting to lash the hurricane lamp to the mast, he had dropped it overboard. I remember thinking what an idiot, but I said something like, *"Don't worry, Alf, we can replace the lamp tomorrow, I could do with another cuppa...."*

I can only say that concentrating on keeping the *Endeavour* on course, staring at the compass and ahead into a cloak of darkness, trying to present the personality of a calm skipper when conversing with Bob and Alf — all at the same time — was beginning to take a toll on me. I breathed a sigh of relief when the alarm rattled in my right ear. I knocked both engines out of gear and told Bob to stop both. The fog remained so thick that I noticed the masthead light looked hazy. I went on deck, cupped my ears and listened in all directions. There were no engine sounds, no seagulls crying, no sound of the Looe fog horn and no sounds of waves on rocks or a shore. Nothing but an eerie silence, except for the lapping of the sea against the *Endeavour*'s planking. I had no idea where we were — not a clue! I guessed we were farther off the land so we could pass safely to the south'ard of Looe Island. I had already dismissed the idea of trying the risky navigation of the narrow channel between Looe Island and the Hannafore mainland to get to Looe harbour.

I told Bob to start both engines again. I put them in gear and came around to course east by north. After another 20 minutes, I repeated the operation: stop engines and listen. I thought I could hear something, so I climbed up on the foredeck and listened. I remember thinking I know that sound – joy! I could hear a faint rhythmic bing-bong, bing-bong. The bell buoy. It had to be the Knight Errant Bell Buoy that marked the Sherbetary Rocks, a ridge of rocks off Downderry (a village a few miles along the coast to the east of Looe). I climbed down off the deck, thanking God, and with a bit of bravado, I remember saying, *"It's okay, I know where we are now. Start 'em up again, Bob."*

A further ten minutes north-northeast, we stopped the engines and went up on deck to listen. The bing-bong, bing-bong, was louder. *"Start 'em up again, Bob."* Another 10 minutes north-northeast, and the engines were cut off again. We were close to the bell buoy. "*Start 'em up again, Bob.*" I altered course to nor' west. After another ten minutes, we stopped the engines again. Bing-bong, bing-bong. The bell buoy was astern on the starboard quarter. Hallelujah, I could hear the intermittent growling sound of the foghorn situated on the western side of the entrance to Looe Harbour. "Start up the Bolinder Bob." Slow ahead, course nor' west. Bob got on the foredeck, listened for the foghorn and guided me by shouting instructions through the wheelhouse window. I caught a glimpse of a red flash of the pier-head light. I was too far to the east of the harbour. Slow ahead until the *Endeavour* came into the flashing white light beam; at first sight, we were almost under the round of the Banjo Pier. As we entered the harbour mouth, I could see my mother walking back along the pier. Apparently, she had been waiting for some time until we arrived safely back in the harbour. This was nothing unusual: if she was not at work, she would often wait on the Banjo Pier until my father was safely in the harbour if he was at sea in bad weather.

We landed our meagre catch of seven stone of pilchards, moved the *Endeavour,* and secured her in a lower quay berth and stopped the '30'. The leg was shipped up, and after a quick scrub down of the deck, my first eventful trip as skipper was at an end. The old, blue, rusted clock showed 10:50 p.m.Nine hours and twenty minutes had elapsed since I had taken command of the *Endeavour*. I stepped ashore that evening with a great feeling of relief and quiet satisfaction that the *Endeavour* was tied up, safe and sound after an eventful trip.

As Looe Harbour Commissioner, I have researched the Looe Harbour archives and obtained access to the Looe Harbour Master's (Arthur Hosking) record of pilchard landings for Sunday, 14 November 1954, to confirm my memory of that day. The record, written in pencil, shows the total landings from the 25 drifters which went to sea that day from Looe (including the Endeavour) was a paltry 260 stones of pilchards to the value of £39 17s 6d (our catch of 7 stone was worth 19s3d). *The largest catch was 78 stones landed by the drifter John Wesley. 15 boats of the 25 failed to make a sale!* This was typical winter "drifting" for Pilchards.

I related the events of the trip to my father, who was still bedridden. In his usual casual way, all I remember of the conversation was him saying, *"Ah, well, ne'er mind, boy, it'll be a better day tamorra'."*

Chapter 13: Another Week

With my father was still unwell, I continued as skipper; I was in my element for the whole of the following week. My ambition fulfilled, Nina was unhappy that I was absent from college, although we had some time together during the week. This wasn't a rehearsal — I was skipper of the *Endeavour*, and I had a gut instinct that Bob and Leggy had the utmost faith in me after the fog episode. We sailed together from the following day, Monday, 15 November 1954, each day up to, and including, Saturday, 20 November 1954, when my father was well enough to resume work.

We missed out completely on Monday evening, hauling the half-mile of net for only a few pilchards, so we returned to the harbour with not enough fish to make a sale. Great disappointment! This was the reality of fishing, and as my Uncle Jack once remarked..."***The reward from fishing is either a gold watch or a raggedy-ass!"*** That evening whilst we were mooring the *Endeavour*, David Pengelly, an electrician who worked in Devonport Dockyard and whose father owned the lugger *Our Daddy*, told me he had a message for me from the Head of the Torpedo Depot; I was to report the next morning to the Main Torpedo Office, which was situated just inside the Albert Road Gate of Devonport Dockyard. I was amazed that my absence had caused such a furore in high places, but I was so wrapped up in my newly found skipper's exploits that no way was I going anywhere until my father was well enough to go back to sea again. I thanked David for passing on the message, and that was that! I kept my own counsel and didn't tell my parents or Nina; if I had, the outcome would have been a foregone conclusion: I would have been packed off back to Plymouth.

During the week, although the weather was fine, the shoals of pilchards were few and far between. Boats searched as far east as Plymouth Sound and Bigbury Bay, to the south of Eddystone Lighthouse and as far west as Falmouth Bay. Never was the saying ***'The luck of the draw'*** more relevant. Some days the odd boat had a decent catch; however, more often than not, most Looe boats drew a blank and struggled to earn a week's wages for their crews. To me, at that time, every trip was exciting as AJ's words '*The great uncertainty*' were never truer. This was just fun to me and was nothing to do with earning that week's wages to keep a family in food and clothing. It was an adventure for me: searching for the fish, catching the fish and landing the fish. Later in life, I was to learn what the strain was like for a fishing boat skipper — trying to continually catch enough fish to feed my own and my crew's families and pay the mortgages on our homes.

Remarkably, Bob and Leggy appeared to accept me as skipper and never questioned my approach to the job at hand.

There was never a query as to what course we took on leaving Looe every afternoon. Each of us did our own thing: Bob looked after the engines, Leggy kept the cabin stove fire going, the kettle full for plenty of mugs of tea, and they left all the other decisions up to me. I can only reiterate that the week I spent with Bob and Leggy taught me a lot. Especially the patience necessary to keep steaming all over the ocean in search of the elusive pilchard shoals.

Each night, I had a debrief from my father: what did we catch, where did we shoot the nets, what was the weather like, which boats caught what and so on. My proudest moment came on the night of Tuesday, 16 November 1954, when I was able to tell my father that we had the second biggest pilchard catch of the Looe fleet. We landed 98 stones and were only beaten by the lugger *Iris* which landed 101 stones. The *Iris* carried a crew of six with a fleet of 14 nets — twice the length of the *Endeavour*'s fleet. I even convinced myself that mathematically we were the top boat for that night when considering the number of nets carried by the other boats in the Looe fleet.

After almost 70 years, my memory of that week is still indelible in my brain because of the frustration I felt. I had failed. This was my big opportunity, but the scarcity of pilchards did not help me prove to my father that I was wasting my time at college. To confirm my recollections, I checked Arthur Hosking's record of pilchard landings held in the Looe Harbour Archives. The *Endeavour*'s landings for the week I was skipper:

Sunday 14th.........................7 stones

Monday15th........................nil

Tuesday 16th.......................98 stones

Wednesday17th.................62 stones

Thursday 18th.....................nil

Friday 19th..........................1 stone

Saturday 20th.....................14 stones

I am sure that in the following years, when I eventually owned fishing boats, the reason I didn't have any problems hiring a crew originated from that one week in November 1954 along with the respect that I gave and was returned to me by Bob and Leggy.

Chapter 14: The Reckoning

All good things have to come to an end, and I returned to Plymouth on Sunday, 21 November, with the 'baggage' of a lot of explaining to do. First to the landlady, who was quite angry until I appeased her by paying the rent for the previous week from which I was absent? I reported to Mr Bill Manley, the foreman of the torpedo depot, at 8:00 a.m. on Monday. He made it perfectly clear that I could be in breach of my Deeds of Apprenticeship, and I would also forfeit a week's wages. (That was no big deal; my pay was £1 2s 5d per week.) I appealed to Mr Manley's sentimentality; after I explained the circumstances of my absence — my father's debilitating 'illness' — the crew of the Endeavour earning no wages if my father remained indisposed etc............ And after due consideration, he relented and just gave me a verbal warning. I went through the same routine with the Vice Principal of the engineering college. This time my reward was a long lecture on reliability, punctuality, plus a large dose of extra course work and the threat of immediate expulsion should I go AWOL again. The next time I was home, both my parents wanted to know if I had gotten into trouble; I "*lied by omission*" I just told them that I was given the extra homework. Looking back over the years to the events of that week, I suppose I got off extremely lightly from my employer. However, faced with the same scenario,

I would do it all over again. Well, perhaps not now…at my age!

The winter of 1954/1955 was not without further drama for me. Just before Christmas, the Dockyard Welfare Section re housed the four of us who lodged at Keppel Street. The reason was not apparent; although, it was not a very "homely" environment, and none of us were very happy staying there. Colin Rowe and I were transferred to 15 Royal Navy Avenue, Keyham. This was the home of Mr and Mrs Byrne, where Colin and I shared one of the four bedrooms.

Following the lodging house upheaval and my November escapade with the *Endeavour*, whilst walking to college in February 1955, I collapsed suffering from a burst appendix and was incarcerated in Plymouth Greenbank Hospital for three weeks. It took me several weeks to recuperate; however, my aim was to get the *Seahorse* back in the water by May.

As an apprentice and student at the engineering college, my working/college week consisted of 44 hours. My paid annual leave entitlement was 88 hours (two weeks) with an additional arbitrary 88 hours unpaid. I arranged to have my annual leave entitlement, paid and unpaid, during the college summer holiday of 1955, which consisted of the last two weeks of July and the first two weeks in August.

During weekends, I worked on repainting the *Seahorse* and overhauling the engine in the marine engineering shop.

Thanks once again to the help and generosity of Ken Newton. It took me until the middle of June to get the *Seahorse* in the water, and I did a deal with Harry Hocking similar to the previous summer. I would have the use of his crab pots in return for selling all my daily catch to him.

My recall of those four weeks is somewhat blurred, they came and went, the weather was fine, and I recollect working the same number of pots, 48 in six strings of eight, as the previous summer, and Nina still freaked out each time we caught a spider crab (skerry). Over the four weeks, my finances took a welcome boost as daily trading my shellfish to Harry Hocking was very successful. My father also gave me a 60-fathom, 12-inch mesh cotton ray (tangle) net, which was laid along the seabed for the main purpose of catching rays, but there was always a side catch of monkfish, turbot, cock crabs, crayfish, etc. I also found the net was lethal for catching skerries.

One episode stands out in my memory. On the first day of my holiday, I was keen to use the ray net, so I shot it in the shallow water of a small sandy stretch beneath the cliffs locally known as Newdrourk, to the east of Looe between Seaton and Downderry, before hauling my crab pots. It was usual to leave the net down for at least three days, so at first light, after three days, I motored to Newdrourk. In the shallow water, it was never a problem for me to haul the ray net. But this morning, after I had picked up the marker Dhan and hauled aboard the end weight, the net was far heavier than I had experienced. In fact, I struggled to haul it up, and all I could see was a tangle of skerries when the end of the net came in sight. They were tangled as far as I could see along the length of the net in the water. I struggled for a while but soon realised I needed help to retrieve it. I cleared a small piece of the net from the skerries that I had aboard. Then I shot the end of the net, Dhan line and Dhan back in the water. I motored back to Looe and asked my father if he could help. Without any hesitation, he came out with me, and between the two of us, we managed to haul the net. I said between *us*, but my father did all the hauling whilst I stowed the net in such a way to keep the *Seahorse* on an even keel. By the time we boarded the net with a huge catch of skerries, a few monkfish, thornback rays and crabs, the *Seahorse* was 'bends to water' (the local name for overloaded). We motored slowly back to Looe. My father helped me for a while to clear some of the nets of skerries, but he left me in the afternoon to finish on my own. He was going pilchard drifting that evening. When I finished clearing the net, as it was made of cotton, the skerries had really made a mess of it. It was difficult to un- mesh a skerry without ripping the net where each one was tangled. It took me many hours of mending to get it ready to shoot again. The skerries at that time were un-saleable, so I took a couple home to eat and dumped the remainder, which were dead, outside the harbour. I remember Harry Hocking paid me £4 10s 0d for the catch — it was equivalent to four weeks of my apprentice wages. (Never be poor, no more!)

With the advent of the United Kingdom later joining the European Economic Community (at first, referred to as the European Common Market), there was a demand for the skerry (spider crab) on the continent. This opened up a new export market and a welcome boost for shell fishermen, who are now getting prices of between 70p and £1.00 per kilo for live skerries, depending on the season.

My four weeks' holiday was over, but there was still about a month to mid-September before my second college year began. Because of the money I earned from the *Seahorse*, I could afford to travel home each weekend and use the *Seahorse* until the new college term started. At the end of September 1955, I put the *Seahorse* in the store for another winter.

Chapter 15: A Disappointing Season and Engagement

Once again, in the spring of 1956, I prepared the *Seahorse* ready for sea, and I took my two weeks paid and two weeks unpaid holiday in July/August. I had the same deal as the previous two summers with Harry Hocking: I would have the use of his pots in return for all the shellfish I caught. I know I negotiated the price of lobsters to be 2s 6d per lb, but I can't recall the price of crabs. That first week when my leave began is etched in my memory. I was extremely excited. I worked really hard to get 48 pots ready, and by the following Monday, I had the six strings of eight pots fishing in various places around Looe Island.

I chose Looe Island because I had information from Harry Hocking that Bill Dove, an astute shell fisherman from West Looe who regularly fished the island area, was landing several lobsters. The weather turned nasty toward the weekend; my pots were in the worst place they could be around the island for a south-westerly gale. I had to wait several days before the sea had calmed enough for me to venture close to the island rocks. The strings of pots were devastated. Even now, after almost 60 years, I can recollect the utter despair a `crabber` feels when hauling pots after a gale of wind has subsided. No string had escaped damage; some pots were in pieces, and very few were still intact. I knew there was only one thing to do —get all the strings ashore to see what could be salvaged. It took me all day to do just that. The hardest part was me having to tell Harry Hocking about the number of his pots that were lost or damaged. I can only remember, with amazement, his reply! He said that I was not to worry and to go and take whatever pots I wanted from his store as replacements. That is exactly what I did. I didn't bother to mend the damaged pots; I just put them in Mr Hocking's store and replaced them with sound ones. I thought at the time I could repair them, in my spare time, at my leisure.

I replenished each of the six strings and got them fishing in the next few days, and during the next couple of weeks, the weather remained fine enough for me to haul the pots every day. But at the beginning of my last week's leave, another unseasonal gale devastated the Looe shell fishermen's pots, including mine. Or should I say Harry Hocking's pots? Actually, Mr Hocking was quite blasé about the destruction of his pots after I salvaged what I could from the six strings. That was the end of the potting season for me, and sadly the last time Mr Hocking and I were in partnership. The end of August 1956 was the finish of a disappointing potting season for me, and I housed the *Seahorse* for the winter in a store on the lower quay that my father had rented off the Looe Harbour Commissioners. The lease had expired on the store in the Albatross building, which was subsequently demolished by the landlord, East Looe Town Trust.

I returned to college in September 1956, disinterested in my education as usual, with my thoughts firmly fixed on the following summer's crabbing season and my career as a fisherman. However, events took a turn during the winter months. College studies at night school became more demanding, and, as I was the sole electrical apprentice in the torpedo department, my superior was putting pressure on me to do well in these studies; moreover, in the departmental exchanges. Nothing would go down better than me obtaining higher exam grades than apprentices from the other departments. A scheme was introduced by the Admiralty where top apprentices could be upgraded to Student Apprentice status. By accepting the position of Student Apprentice, I was informed I would be guaranteed the post of a basic grade draughtsman at the end of my five-year apprenticeship without taking the draughtsman exam. In the two years I spent at the engineering college, the only subject that interested me was technical drawing, so this opportunity seemed too good to turn down. As electrical draughtsmen were as scarce as hen's teeth in the torpedo department, I accepted the position as Student Apprentice.

Nina and I became engaged to be married at Christmas 1956. She was 18 years old, and I was 19. I remember Nina's mother was friendly with the owner of the Westwell Jewel

Company, jewellers, which was situated on the Royal Parade in Plymouth. Nina chose a second-hand beautiful solitaire diamond ring which the jeweller let me have for the knockdown price of £80. (We later insured the ring for £500.)

Chapter 16: Uncle Fred, Licensing and Wedding Plans

In the spring of 1957, as the last of their five sons had left home, Mr and Mrs Byrne relinquished their corporation house in Royal Navy Avenue, so we moved to 391 Wolseley Road, a three-bedroom, World War II prefabricated building (locally known as "***Prefab`s***) in the Camels Head district of Plymouth. The `prefab` was situated next to the Camels Head Sewage Works, and one could certainly smell it when the wind was in a certain direction!

(A prefab was a prefabricated building manufactured offsite in advance and used extensively in Plymouth during World War II to re-house families that had been "bombed out". They remained inhabited for many years after the war.)

With the change in my status, I found more of my spare time was taken up with study and was struggling to find time on alternate weekends to prepare the *Seahorse* ready for the summer. I had already booked my usual holiday for the last two weeks in July and the first two weeks in August 1957, and eventually, I got the *Seahorse* in the harbour by the beginning of July. As I didn't have the backup of Mr Hocking's resources, I decided to spend more of my holiday trawling and ray netting as well as shooting the few old pots we had in store. It was a good thing that I had decided to change my mode of fishing because, at the end of my first week's leave, there were gales and torrential rain. The August weather was no better than those in the last days of July. I have recollections of the bad weather and being caught in a terrific thunderstorm whilst trawling in Whitsand Bay — scary. On the whole, thinking back to that time, my four weeks' leave was a disaster. The *Seahorse* spent more time moored alongside the quay than it did out at sea.

Uncle Fred Lewis

My Uncle Fred Lewis owned and hired out, by the hour to visitors, a fleet of self-drive motorboats. These were known locally as '*doodlebugs*'. He suggested I get a licence for the *Seahorse* so she could be hired out and share the proceeds fifty-fifty. I applied to Looe Urban District Council, the licensing authority, and received an annual licence (No 954, which I still have) for the *Seahorse* to carry eight passengers, dated 22 July 1957 and was valid until 30 June 1958. I agreed that Uncle Fred would take care of and hire out the *Seahorse* when I was in Plymouth. This arrangement was successful for the last period of August, and the cash I received for my share was very welcome. The *Seahorse* was put away in the store by the time my new college term started in September.

My extra studies must have been noticed in high places because I received a letter from the Deputy Armament Supply Officer (Torpedo), dated 15 August 1957, congratulating me on my improved results for the midsummer term. I found the third year at college more intense than either of the two previous years; however, I recall one item of interest. There were several lessons on the design of the ship's propellers. This stood me in good stead because in 1976, I had my 38ft trawler *Corinthian* (FY405), built by Gerald Pearn, and I had an input into the design of the propeller to suit the gearbox for the six-cylinder Mercedes Diesel engine installed in the boat.

Nina and I fixed our wedding date for 23 March 1959 as I would be nearing the end of my apprenticeship.

Once again, I booked my usual four weeks' leave for July/August 1958. With the added pressure to do well at college during the 1958 summer semester, I found it difficult to get much work done to prepare the *Seahorse* for that summer season. After a discussion with Uncle Fred, he suggested that I should apply for a licence to take passengers on fishing trips to add to my licence to operate on the ferry. This I did, and on the 30 June 1958, I passed the requisite test in front of the then Looe Harbour Master, Mr Jack Sargent, to gain my licence to take passengers outside Looe harbour within the designated limits: two miles south of Looe (Seaton Beach to the east and Orestone to the west).

During my four weeks' leave, I worked a few crab pots, and for the first two weeks, I took visitors angling within the permitted limits of my personal licence. I knew after a few days that taking visitors angling was not my forte. I could not abide the rudeness of some treating me as some illiterate yokel, their whingeing and whining if we didn't catch any fish, and those with their *superior knowledge* in the field of sea angling. That was the first and last time I took paying passengers on angling trips in the Seahorse. For the last two weeks of my leave, I went to sea early in the morning to haul my pots and then allowed Uncle Fred to hire the *Seahorse* along with his doodlebugs for the rest of the day. As Nina and I were now getting married, the money was very welcome because my apprentice weekly wage was still meagre.

My leave passed quickly; looking back, it was the least amount of time I spent with the *Seahorse* since she was built. It was during this period that I realised, with all the things going on in my life at the time, my dream of becoming a fisherman needed to be put on the back burner. It was with a heavy heart that I stored the *Seahorse* for another winter.

Harbour Documents

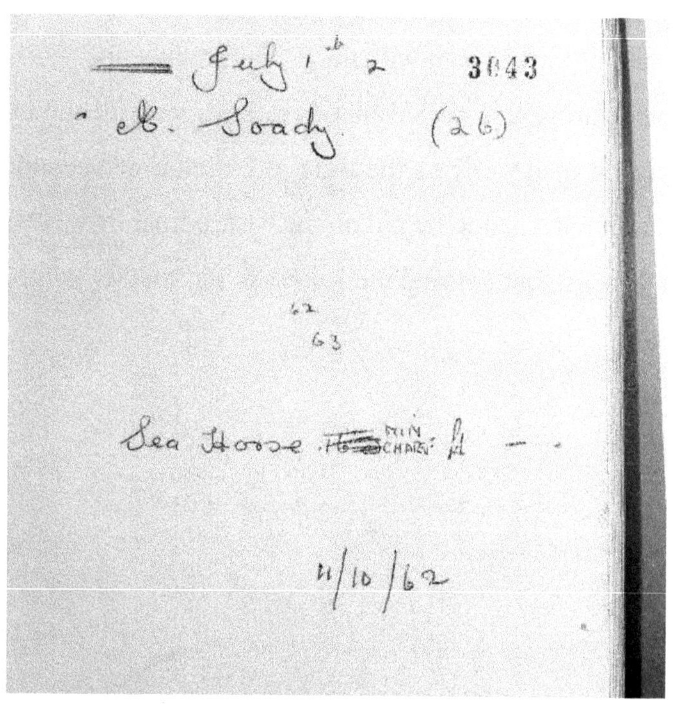

July 1st 2 3643

M. Soady (26)

62
63

Sea Horse MIN CHARGE £1 - -

11/10/62

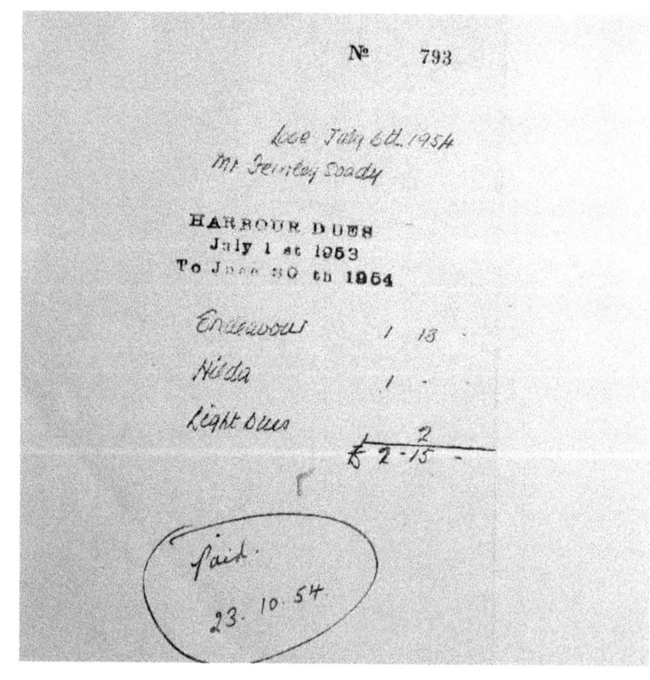

№ 793

Looe July 6th 1954

Mr Fernley Soady

HARBOUR DUES
July 1st 1953
To June 30th 1954

Endeavour	1 13 -
Hilda	1 - -
Light Dues	2
	£2-15-

Paid.
23. 10. 54

41-

No.

LOOE URBAN DISTRICT COUNCIL

LICENCE FOR PLEASURE BOATS

The Looe Urban District Council hereby License until the 30th day of June, 19[illegible], the pleasure boat(s) or vessel(s) belonging to

Mr. Michael Scally

of Lower Chapel Street Looe

and described as follows:

No.	Description	Name	Length	No. of Passengers not to exceed
	Motor Launch	Sea Horse	16'	8

to be let for hire, or to be used for carrying Passengers for hire, subject to the conditions in the Bye-laws of the Council duly confirmed by the Minister of Health.

Dated this 22nd *day of* July 19[illegible]

Clerk of the Council.

A. N. Hosking

Harbour Master.

NOTE.—This Licence may be revoked or suspended whenever the

Restricted 2 mls S of Looe, Seaton Beach to E & Oreston to W.

No. 712

LOOE URBAN DISTRICT COUNCIL

WATERMAN'S PERSONAL LICENCE

Mr. [illegible]

of [illegible]

is hereby licensed until the 30th day of June, 19[illegible], as a waterman in charge of a boat in the following category or categories licensed by the above named Council to ply for hire within the jurisdiction of the Urban District of Looe.

Categories of Waterman's Licences

(a) ~~Rowing Boat.~~
(b) ~~Sailing Boat.~~
(c) Motor Boat—Maximum Speed *not exceeding* 15 knots.
(i) Length of boat not exceeding 18-ft. and rating of engine not exceeding 3 h.p.
(ii) ~~Length of boat not exceeding 18-ft. and rating of engine exceeding 3 h.p.~~
(iii) ~~Length of boat exceeding 18-ft. and rating of engine not exceeding 3 h.p.~~
(iv) ~~Length of boat exceeding 18-ft. and rating of engine exceeding 3 h.p.~~
(d) ~~Motor Boat—Maximum Speed *exceeding* 15 knots.~~

Dated this 30 day of June 195[illegible]

Clerk of the Council.

Harbour Master.

NOTE.—This Licence may be revoked or suspended whenever the Council considers it necessary or desirable.

Looe Harbour Records Harbour Dues 1947

	Owner	Name	Description	Length	Pass.	Rate	£	s	d	Remarks	Paid
	Scady Tomley	Endeavour	motor launch	31' 3"	12	9	1	8	3	Sold to St Ives Left Port 26.9.47	
		Hilda	Punt	13'	5 persons			4	6		
		Light Dues						2			
							1	5	8		4.7.47
		Endeavour II	motor launch	35' 3"		9		6	8	Launched by [illegible] April 27th 1947 [illegible]	

	Owner	Name	Description	Length	Pass.	Rate	£	s	d	Remarks
	[illegible]	[illegible]	motor launch	28'	12	9		16	6	
		[illegible]	Punt	13'	5 persons			7	6	
		Light Dues						1		
							1	5	0	
	Symons Tomley	[illegible]	motor Punt	14'		9		14		Sold [illegible] 1939 [illegible]
	Seccombe W.	Banshee	Punt	14'		9		14		[illegible]
	Sharland J.B.	[illegible]	Punt	14'		9		14		
34	Scady Tomley	Endeavour	motor launch	31'	12	9	1	3	3	[illegible]
		Hilda	Punt	13	5 persons					
		Light Dues						2		
							1	5	8	
121	Symons Sam	Golden Fleece	Rowing	16'	8	9		12		

1938 — 1939

	Name	Name	Description	Length	Pass.	Rate	£ s. d.	Remarks
	[illegible] Sam.	Golden Star	Motor Launch	22'	12	9	16 6	
		Iris	Punt	13'	6 persons		7 6	
		Light Dues					1 -	
							£ 1 5 0	
	Symons Jemley	Met	Motor Punt	14'		1/-	14	Sold Xmas 1939 See Blake E.R.
	Seccombe W.	Banshee	Punt	14'		1/-		
	Sharland J.E.	Shed	Punt	14'		1/-	14 -	
34	Scady Jemley	Endeavour	Motor Launch	31'	12	9	1 3 3	[illegible]
		Hilda	Punt	13	5 persons			
		Light Dues					2	
							£ 1 - 5 - 3	
21	Symons Sam.	Golden Fleece	Rowing	16'	8	9	12 -	

Chapter 17: HMS Collingwood and a Wedding

Our wedding day, 21 March 1959

In early November 1958, I was informed by the Superintending Armament Supply Officer, R N Armament Depot, Bull Point, Plymouth, that I was to report to HMS Collingwood at Fareham, Hampshire, on 5 December 1958 to attend a nine-month educational course which included ship radio communication, radar and guided weapon control. I was to board in the No.5 Petty Officers Mess. This was a bolt from the blue for Nina and me. We had arranged to be married on 23 March 1959; being drafted to HMS Collingwood meant we had to change the arrangements for our wedding.

I duly took up my position at HMS Collingwood and, after initially travelling by train to Fareham, I hitched a regular fortnightly lift from Looe to Fareham and back in a split windscreen Morris Minor. I'm afraid that is my only recollection of those journeys. I have no idea who was the owner/driver or the name of the other passenger who travelled with me; however, I enjoyed the course, and I still have fond recollections of the camaraderie I received from all the Petty Officers in that mess. I was even allocated a daily rum ration, although I was a civilian who, like several others, I saved my ration until the weekends that I had to stay on board. I have to reveal that because of those weekend binges, I now have an intense dislike of rum, even the smell of it.

Nina's mother had moved to Kempsey, Worcestershire, to manage the Ketch Hotel, so we changed our plans and agreed to be married in Worcester. I hired a coach for my mother and father, as well as many of my relatives, to travel from Looe to Kempsey, where that all stayed at the `Ketch`, compliments of Nina`s mother. My best man was National

Service Naval Petty Officer Percy Lawrenson, who hailed from Liverpool. He drove me from Fareham to Kempsey, and I remember when we were about halfway through our journey, Percy pulled into a layby. Stopped the engine and said, "*Well Jan*, (that was my name at `Collingwood`! All Cornishmen were "Janners") *we`re halfway there, do you want to go back? This is your chance to turn around!*" ............. Nina and I were married on 21 March 1959 at St Mark's Church in the Cherry Orchard, Worcester. Nina`s mother, Irene (mother-in-law as I always called her!), put on a first-class reception for Nina, our guests and me, and because the celebration went over time, we missed the train for our honeymoon. Good old Percy came to our rescue and drove us from Kempsey to Lydney. We spent a week on honeymoon at a small village in Gloucestershire called Lydney, then returned to Looe where we rented `Easterleigh`, a cottage from my parents, in Lower Chapel Street, East Looe; the cottage where I had spent all my young life prior to lodging in Plymouth. My parents had moved into the guest house "Sea Breeze", Lower Chapel Street, which they had constructed on the site of two derelict cottages.

The course was adjourned for a fortnight, so I applied to take my 88 hours (two weeks) paid leave from Collingwood up to 1 May 1959, as I didn't want to spend two weeks in Plymouth back in the torpedo depot. During those two weeks, I prepared the *Seahorse*, launched her and left her in the capable hands of Uncle Fred, who had agreed to hire her to visitors again during the summer.

I completed my course at HMS Collingwood on 7 August 1959. I applied for and was granted my 88 hours unpaid leave from Monday, 10 August 1959, to Friday, 21 August, which I spent working the *Seahorse*; mainly trawling, long lining for conger and ray, and with one string of eight crab pots when the weather was kind. There were gale-force winds from the south and southwest during the last three days of my first week. Actually, as far as I recall, because of the bad weather, the small amount of prime fish that I caught trawling —turbot, brill, Dover sole and plaice — made sky-high prices. By the end of my two weeks' leave, I had earned more money than Uncle Fred hiring out the *Seahorse* for self-drive to visitors in the same time period; however, he carried on hiring the *Seahorse* for self-drive until I had the time to put the boat into winter storage in September.

I reported to the North Yard Torpedo Depot on 24 August 1959, somewhat relieved that my sojourn at HMS Collingwood was over because I was now a married man and only getting home from Fareham to my new wife every other weekend was no fun. On my arrival at the Depot, I was informed by Bill Manley that I was to take up my appointment as a confirmed Electrical Draughtsman, and he ordered me to report to the Electrical Drawing Office, Devonport Dockyard, on 7 September 1959 for a six month period to gain experience. At that time, I remember thinking that I had become one of a small, elite group of electrical draughtsmen attached to the Armament Supply Department. This was tinged with regret. The thought of my boyhood aspiration of becoming a fisherman was fading. I also harboured grave doubts as to how much time I would have to use the *Seahorse,* as I would be working full time in the drawing office. However, my negative thoughts were tempered somewhat when I learned that as a draughtsman, I was entitled to 20 days of paid leave each year (4 weeks).

Chapter 18: A Shock

During my five years Admiralty training, I had spent four years at College and studied, amongst other subjects, Mathematics and Applied Mathematics to degree level for those four years (*I did not wish to attend university.*); attaining Pure and applied maths `A` level and a National Certificate in Mechanical Engineering, I spent my first year in the machine shop, being trained in `bench work` and the second year as a trainee lathe operator, which was great. I was even thought good enough to be employed on naval contract work, turning out thousands of various sizes in threaded bolts for use aboard ship, for which I was paid extra. (This was termed "contract money"). My third year was spent as a junior member (a "gofer") of a three-man shipboard "gang"; comprising an electrical fitter, a labourer and me. I really liked the work, mainly fixing "carrier plate" for electric cable, ripping out and replacing the old and obsolescent wiring on His Majesty`s warships. I enjoyed all my time working on the various warships; the frigate HMS "Loch Fyne", the aircraft carrier HMS "Eagle" and the smallest "S" Class submarine in the British Navy, HMS "Scotsman". My favourite was the time I spent helping to rewire the Admirals cabin aboard the cruiser HMS "Belfast"; which is now moored in the river Thames. The time in my fourth year, as well as being my last year in College, was spent part-time in the North Yard Torpedo Depot (where, as a personal project, I had permission to and actually constructed a fully working valve wireless) and latterly in the main Electrical Drawing Office, Devonport, where I was instructed into drawing layouts, electrical wiring diagrams etc. for ships.

On the completion of my 5-year" apprenticeship, I was given the full-time position of Electrical Draughtsman under the auspices of the Admiralty Superintendant Armament Supply Officer, (SASO) Devonport and situated in the Guided Weapons Drawing Office at R.N.A.D Ernesettle, Plymouth. I was the sole Electrical Draughtsman for the (SASO) at Plymouth. When I mentioned National Service to the SASO, I was assured that I had a "restricted" job and I would never be "called up" for National Service.

Much to my surprise, it turned out after a short while that I thoroughly enjoyed my work in the Electrical Drawing Office; thoughts of being a Fisherman had drifted from my mind. I found that I was good at the job, and the Chief Draughtsman must have recognised this because I was soon allocated work similar to the longstanding electrical draughtsmen. Sad to say, after being accepted and befriended in the drawing office, my time there was destined to be short-lived. I cannot recall the date, but sometime during October 1959, I received my `call-up` papers to do the statutory two years of Service in the British armed forces.

As a fully qualified Admiralty Electrical Draughtsman working on confidential documents and drawings, I had been assured that I was exempt from conscription. I believe that the Armament Supply Officer of Plymouth challenged the War Department with regard to my `call up`, but his intervention was to no avail. I would have to serve my two years like every other young male over the age of 18.

So much for my "exemption!!!" I travelled to Devonport and passed the medical for the armed services, and shortly after, I was conscripted, not into the Royal Navy, but into the British Army!!!

To me, the decision to conscript me into the Army was absolutely ludicrous; this despite my previous five years of working knowledge and experience with the British Naval vessels. So on 3 February 1960, I travelled by train from Looe and reported to Gibraltar Barracks, Farnborough, the British Army Royal Engineers Training Establishment. On completion of my 12 weeks of basic training at Gibraltar Barracks, I was transferred to the Royal Military Police Training Establishment, Inkerman Barracks at Woking, where I trained as a British Army Military Policeman. After a further 14 weeks of really tough training, I spent the remainder of my National Service as a Non-Commissioned Officer of the Military Police in 158 Provost Company, Company HQ attached to the 7th Armoured Brigade and stationed at Gordon Barracks, Bulford on Salisbury Plain. I was now one of the notorious "Red Caps!!"

During my two years of National Service, the "*Seahorse*" remained in the store.

Nina gave birth to our two eldest daughters, Deborah and Dena, whilst I was serving my two years in the Military Police; I was demobbed and arrived home to Looe late in the evening of 31 January 1962, to a raging storm. Some homecoming? (I arrived with three weeks' paid leave consisting of the princely sum of £9 0s 0d.) Our family financial savings prior to my two years of army service had been completely dissipated and returning to family life. I had to get back to work and start earning a `living` again as soon as I possibly could. I contacted the Assistant Supply Officer at RNAD Ernesettle (who just happened to be my Cousin Bill Soady!), and on 12 February 1962, at the age of 24, I started work as the sole Electrical Draughtsman in charge of all the electrical elements of the Armament Supply Drawing Offices at Ernesettle, Bull Point, and the Royal William Yard (Gun Wharf), Devonport. I had scant knowledge of guns, ammunition, etc., and did not pretend that I did, but what I didn`t know about guns and ammo, I quickly learned from Albert Studden, a long term acting Mechanical Draughtsman, who was at least twice my age. Albert lived in Plymouth, and we soon became firm friends

I had high hopes for the *Seahorse* in the summer of 1962, considering that I had a 20 working day Annual leave entitlement (4 weeks). I spent a lot of my free time refitting the boat, and she was launched on Easter Monday, which was in late April. What I came to realise was that the post I had returned to was important and extremely demanding. There was less and less time for me to use the "Seahorse", and I found difficulty travelling to and from Plymouth to work. Once again, when I was not using the Seahorse for fishing, Uncle Fred hired out the boat, and we split the proceeds fifty-fifty.

Me on leave from the Army, September 1960

Whilst living at home in Looe for the first time in seven and a half years, I had an idea to leave the Seahorse in the harbour all through the winter of 1962 - 1963 so that I could use the boat at weekends. What seemed a good idea proved to be a bad one [This was another of my ideas that should have remained an idea!]. With heavy rainfall and bad weather, I seemed to be spending more time pumping water out of the Seahorse than actually going to sea. Finally, during the Christmas holiday, I put the Seahorse in my Father`s store for the remainder of the winter. It was a good move because a few days after Christmas, as I recall, there were heavy snowfalls throughout the Southwest of England. January 1963 was particularly cold, and I found it quite difficult to travel to and from Plymouth to work. The Seahorse remained safe in my father`s store.

I refitted and put the *Seahorse* in the water on Easter Saturday in 1963. It was a repeat of the previous year. The pressure of my job and bad weather when I had days off work meant I had little time to take the *Seahorse* to sea. Unfortunately, this year, Uncle Fred couldn't manage to hire out the boat for self-drive. For most of the summer, the *Seahorse* became a problem, more than an asset and the boat sadly languished alongside the harbour wall. As much as I hated the thought, I began to foster the idea to put the boat up for sale.

I have no recollection of when I made the decision or how the opportunity came about to sell the *Seahorse* to local doctor John Gates, other than I met with Dr Gates early on Saturday, 8 June 1963. I gave Dr Gates a trial trip in the *Seahorse* around Looe Bay which turned out to be my last trip in the boat.

It was an extremely poignant and sad day for me when I agreed on the sale of the *Seahorse* to Dr Gates for £250. I sold my "old friend!" A sale I regret to this day.

The era of nine years from 1954 to 1963, during which the Seahorse had been a part of my life, was now at an end, and my ambition to be a Fisherman seemed to have turned to `ashes`.

However, as the old saying goes...." When one door closes, another one opens!"

Little did I realise that my life was about to change dramatically three years later, with one phone call on 13 June 1966. The dormant flame which was still inside me to become a Fisherman was about to be reignited....................

www.ingramcontent.com/pod-product-compliance
Ingram Content Group UK Ltd.
Pitfield, Milton Keynes, MK11 3LW, UK
UKHW051207260726
13967UKWH00011B/3145